Making Sense of the Commandments

Making Sense of the Commandments

Rupert E. Davies

EPWORTH PRESS

British Library Cataloguing in Publication Data

Davies, Rupert E. (Rupert Eric)
Making sense of the commandments.
1. Ten commandments – Critical Studies
I. Title
222.1606

ISBN 0–7162–0465–7

First published 1990
by Epworth Press
Room 195, 1 Central Buildings
Westminster London SW1H 9NR

Typeset by Gloucester Typesetting Services
and printed in Great Britain by
Richard Clay Ltd, Bungay, Suffolk

Contents

Preface

No one denies that the Western world is in a state of moral confusion. Old standards have disappeared; new ones are not yet recognized. Moral injunctions come in fusillades from the press and the other media, from advertisers and politicians. But the advice given is highly contradictory, and rings hollow because it proceeds from no fixed principles, except the vaguest (such as 'democracy'), and is often dictated by the financial or party-political interests of the adviser. Meanwhile most people carry on their lives with no particular purpose save that of gaining their own advantage in the activities which appeal to them (though not without some outbursts of generosity and unselfishness).

So I have thought it worthwhile to have another look at the Ten Commandments, for many centuries the foundation of European ethics; and then to see what light is cast on them for our times by the two 'Great Commandments' of Jesus Christ. I believe that the results of these enquiries are positive and relevant to our time, and I set them out in this book. I have tried at all points to unite theory with practice, since in the past ethical theory by itself has proved valueless, and sheer pragmatism has led to gross inconsistency.

I have written, not for Old Testament scholars (though they may question some of my statements), nor especially for scholars of any kind, but for puzzled Christians, and others, of all kinds. I hope that many of them will discuss the book in groups, as people are doing with my earlier *Making Sense of the Creeds*.

The books of biblical scholars have been consulted, and the views of theologians and philosophers considered, but I owe just as much to my friends in many walks of life with whom I have talked about these matters over many years, and most of all to my wife, Margaret, who has read the total manuscript and taken nothing for granted except the all-importance of truth.

Christine Lillington has again triumphed over my illegible hand-writing in typing the manuscript.

There is no index, since the chapter headings should be sufficient to indicate where individual subjects are handled.

Biblical references are to the New English Bible.

Bishopsworth, Bristol   Rupert E. Davies
May 1989

I *Where do the Commandments come from?*

If a man stole the property of temple or state, he shall be put to death; also the one who received the stolen goods from his hand shall be put to death.

If a man has stolen the young son of another man, he shall be put to death.

If a man committed robbery and was caught, he shall be put to death.

If a man's wife has been caught while lying with another man, they shall bind them and throw them into the water. If the woman's husband wishes to spare his wife, then the king may spare his subject.

If a son has struck his father, they shall cut off his hand.

No. These are not the laws of Moses, nor are they found anywhere in the Old Testament. They are part of the 'Code of Hammurabi', and date back centuries before the birth of Moses, perhaps to about 1760 BC. Hammurabi was a great king of Babylon (he describes himself, modestly, as 'the perfect king'), who for a time ruled over Assyria as well (the two countries covered what we now call Iraq); and he consolidated his authority by issuing his code of laws (282 of them). He (or his civil servants and legal advisers) compiled it after consulting several of the other codes (some of which have been unearthed in modern times) which were in force among neighbouring countries.

Centuries later, when Israel was constituted as a nation by the covenant made with Jahweh on Mount Sinai, after the deliverance from Egyptian bondage (perhaps about 1250 BC), Moses and his colleagues saw clearly that a code of laws was needed to guide the life of the nation and maintain good order. The Code of Hammurabi and no doubt other codes were available for inspection, and the result of studying them and the needs of Israel was the publication of the original form of the code contained in Exodus 20, called 'the Ten Words', 'The Decalogue', or 'the Ten Commandments' interchangeably. This was followed over many years by the promulgation of a long series of separate laws for particular areas of life; these are to be found in the Book of Exodus, and those other books of the Pentateuch, little read by Christians, Leviticus, Numbers and Deuteronomy.

The Ten Words and the subsequent regulations, and the penalties incurred by breaking them, are different in many ways from Hammurabi's Code, but the scholars who have made careful comparisons are sure that the two codes, the earlier and the later, belong to the same family of ancient legislation. They are certainly not twins or clones, but they are at least first cousins.

According to Israelitish tradition, embodied in Exodus, the Ten Words were inscribed by Jahweh himself on tablets of stone (presumably in Hebrew), and handed over by him to Moses for enactment (a tradition somewhat oddly preserved in many English churches and chapels by a mural picture of two stone tablets with just the Roman numerals I, II, III, IV etc. inscribed upon them). However this may be, the familiar version of the Decalogue, and the one that we shall use in this book, is in Ex. 20.1–17. It runs like this in the New English Bible:

God spoke, and these were his words:
I am the LORD your God who brought you out of Egypt, out of the land of slavery.
You shall have no other god to set against me.

You shall not make a carved image for yourself nor the likeness of anything in the heavens above, or on the earth below, or in the waters under the earth.

You shall not bow down to them or worship them; for I, the LORD your God, am a jealous god. I punish the children for the sins of the fathers to the third and fourth generation of those who hate me. But I keep faith with thousands, with those who love me and keep my commandments.

You shall not make wrong use of the name of the LORD your God; the LORD will not leave unpunished the man who misuses his name.

Remember to keep the Sabbath day holy. You have six days to labour and do all your work. But the seventh day is a Sabbath of the LORD your God; that day you shall not do any work, you, your son or your daughter, your slave or your slave-girl, your cattle or the alien within your gates; for in six days the LORD made heaven and earth, the sea, and all that is in them, and on the seventh day he rested. Therefore the LORD blessed the Sabbath day and declared it holy.

Honour your father and your mother, that you may live long in the land which the LORD your God is giving you.

You shall not commit murder.

You shall not commit adultery.

You shall not steal.

You shall not give false evidence against your neighbour.

You shall not covet your neighbour's house; you shall not covet your neighbour's wife, his slave, his slave-girl, his ox, his ass, or anything that belongs to him.

But this is not the only version which the Bible provides. There is another, slightly different one in Deut. 5.6–21 (no doubt dating from a somewhat later period), the chief difference being that in Deuteronomy a humanitarian motive – not to work your slaves too hard – is given for the observance of the sabbath, and that coveting one's neighbour's wife is by now apparently regarded as a more serious offence than coveting his house. There is yet another version, or what is virtually a different Decalogue, in Ex. 34.17–26. It was once thought that this was older than our Ten Commandments, but nowadays many people put it at a later date. It is not possible to be sure about this, and different scholars say different things. The name given to this collection of laws is 'the Ritual Decalogue', since it is much more concerned with the performance of ritual acts and the keeping of festivals than with behaviour, and it ends with the famous injunction not to boil a kid in its mother's milk. We do not perhaps need to pay much attention to such instructions.

But can we be sure that the familiar version of the Ten Commandments really goes back to the time of Moses, and that it therefore bears the marks of his personality? The answer is that we cannot. The Decalogue can hardly be Mosaic all the way through, since the command to do no work on the Sabbath could just not be kept by a nomadic people – as the crowd which crossed the Red Sea certainly was – which must look after its animals on every day of the week. It is not even certain that the Hebrews kept the Sabbath at all, or at all strictly, until long after the time of Moses, in fact, not until after contact with the Babylonians many centuries later. And the motive suggested for observing the commandment not to make carved images, which was the fear of being punished to the third and fourth generation, does not make sense for the time of Moses, since images of various sorts were used in worship without official disapproval until the prophets denounced them in the eighth century. (These points will recur when we come to treat the individual commandments).

But it is quite likely that the core of the Decalogue, the Ten Commandments in their simplest form, does go back to Moses, and formed the basis of law on which the Hebrews started their chequered history at Mount Sinai.

This is the early history of the Decalogue as modern research has shown it to us. But some Christians and Jews may object to this account on the ground that it makes the whole thing a very human affair – Moses and his council of elders poring over the legal enactments of other nations, coming up with the laws which they deemed appropriate to their own people, and then claiming divine approval;

and, later, other well-meaning persons adding embellishments and refinements to the original text to help form the Hebrew people into a God-fearing, law-abiding and disciplined community. What has happened to the ancient assurance that God transmitted his will in person to Moses, and saw to it that he did not forget it by inscribing it on stone tablets?

The fact that the giving of the law on Sinai now has to be seen as a 'very human affair' does not make it any less a divine act. For God, in the Christian view, acts with and through his human servants, not taking them over or preserving them from all evil, but helping them to see as clearly as their abilities allow his will for them and for those for whom they have responsibility. And the conviction that this is what happened in the case of the Ten Commandments is amply borne out by the enormous, almost incredible hold that the Ten Commandments have had on human society from the time of Moses until now.

2 How useful have they been?

The Ten Commandments have served as the foundation stone of law for the Hebrews ever since their enactment, both during their short periods of national independence in ancient times, and within the close-knit communities which have preserved their religion and their common life under harsh tyrannies and cultural ostracism in ancient times and ever since. In the modern state of Israel they are still insisted on as valid by the religious parties within the state. The Decalogue is the basis of the Torah, which is the word for Jewish Law in its totality, and must, they say, be honoured as such.

The Ten have at all times needed interpretation, as all laws must; they have needed application to the changing circumstances of national and personal life. We can see the process of intense study and meticulous regulation, which is characteristic of Jewish thought, already at work in the books of the Pentateuch. It was continued, in broader terms, by the prophets of the eighth and later centuries BC, and by their disciples. It was intensified by the rabbis and scribes after the return from Babylonian exile in the sixth century, and resulted in greater and greater complication into the time of Jesus and beyond into the Middle Ages. We can observe signs of the continuing process in the arguments of Jesus with the Pharisees, and in the use of rabbinic learning by Paul in some of his letters, especially Galatians and Romans. And Jewish scholars today can point with great and justifiable pride to the immense accumulation of legal and moral wisdom enshrined in the sayings of the rabbis in century after century.

A notable illustration of the way in which this process of interpretation was carried on is the story of the discovery of the 'Book of the Law' in the Jerusalem Temple in 608 BC (described in II Kings 22.1–13). It was in the time of the good king Josiah, and the Book was hailed by its finders, and accepted by the king, as the long-lost work of Moses. Probably it is much the same as the Book of Deuteronomy, which cannot be Moses' work since it describes his death. It is very likely that Josiah's priestly advisers, with the best motives, had hidden the Book in the Temple with a view to its being 'discovered' a little later on. It seemed to them to embody the teaching of Moses, and they wanted his authority for it.

It was rapidly enacted by the king as God's law, and gave a new perspective to many ancient rules and regulations. For it insisted that Jahweh was the only god in the entire universe, whereas up till then the existence of other gods had not been officially denied, though the prophets had fiercely contended for such a denial. It also laid down that sacrifice to Jahweh could be offered in Jerusalem, and nowhere else (that is, not in the numerous shrines up and down the kingdom). The Book also made it clear that those who obeyed its precepts would prosper, and those who did not, would not (this applied to the king as well as to the citizenry).

So the Ten Commandments, without losing their authority, had acquired an important codicil. And in spite of all the sophistication of the interpretative process from then until now the solid base of the Decalogue has never been tampered with. Jesus could appeal to it on the common ground between himself and the Rich Young Ruler (Mark 10.14). And, no doubt, when secular Israelis discuss moral and legal issues in the bars and bistros of modern Tel Aviv, they start from the common assumption that it is built into their national history.

When the Romans took over the rule of the Mediterranean world, they brought the whole area within the scope of their own elaborate legal system, but allowed some local variations according to the traditions of each city and country, so long as the framework of Roman law was not breached. The rise and growth of Christianity presented some difficult problems to Roman provincial governors, and later to the Emperors themselves; for here were people who claimed to obey Roman law so far as it was just and right, but appealed to a higher law when they thought it was not. Hence the persecution of Christians, which continued intermittently until the reign of Constantine at the beginning of the fourth century AD.

After Christianity had been legalized by Constantine, and made the official religion of the Empire by his successors, it became necessary to reconcile Roman law and 'Christian' law, which included the Ten Commandments. This was done by distinguishing civil (i.e. Roman) law from ecclesiastical (i.e. Christian) law, and the reconciliation was consummated by the Code of the Emperor Justinian, published in 529. Justinian's lawyers produced an amalgam of Roman law and the Bible; they defined the authority of the Emperor and his law enforcement officers as concerned with human affairs; and the authority of the Christian priesthood as concerned with divine affairs. The two authorities were to be regarded as interdependent, and neither was subordinate to the other.

The moral law was not at this point clearly distinguished from the law of the state or the law of the church, but it tended to come under the law of the church. In mediaeval times this tendency was confirmed; the state punished criminals in its own way, the church punished moral delinquents in its own non-violent way. Heretics furnished a difficulty, since they were thought to break all the laws of both church and state. In the days of the Holy Inquisition the church tried them, found them guilty and pronounced eternal damnation; it then handed them over to 'the secular arm' to punish them, preferably by burning them. The atmosphere of those times is vividly, and not inaccurately, described in Umberto Eco's novel *The Name of the Rose*.

Since the Reformation the distinction between *three* kinds of law has become current in European and North American states (not in Muslim countries, as we have been reminded very forcefully by Ayatollah Khomeini). The three are the civil law; the ecclesiastical (or canon) law; the moral law. The three overlap and interact quite considerably from time to time, but they can be thought about and discussed separately.

The distinction between the moral law and the civil law was first made really clear in Britain by the famous Wolfenden Report on Homosexuality in 1957. The Report distinguished between immorality and crime, and recommended that homosexual acts in private between consenting adult males should no longer be punishable by law, since they belonged to the sphere of morals and not of law. So we can now see that what is immoral is often not criminal (e.g. adultery): and that what is illegal is often not immoral (e.g. refusal to give up one's Christian faith in an atheist country).

So far as the *civil* law is concerned the Decalogue has now only a small part to play. All civilized countries have laws prohibiting theft, murder and perjury. But they do not need the Ten Commandments to tell them what they are to do about these. There are laws about Sunday observance, based on the Commandment 'to keep holy the Sabbath Day' (on the assumption, not entirely justified, that Sunday and the Sabbath are the same), on the statute books of most countries where Christianity is the chief religion; but, as we know from our own country, their force has been steadily eroded, and it may not be long before it disappears altogether in Britain and elsewhere. Anti-blasphemy laws no doubt come indirectly from the Commandment not 'to take the name of the Lord in vain', and they retain into modern times the residue of a religious sentiment: but mostly they are concerned with not offending human beings by outraging their beliefs. Adultery has long since ceased to be a penal offence.

There is a closer connexion between the Decalogue and *ecclesiastical* law. Most churches, at least officially, regard a serious breach of any of the Ten Commandments as a cause for disciplinary action; and the Commandments are included in the liturgies of the Church of England, the Methodist Church and other churches. This must be taken to imply that they are laid upon church members as a solemn obligation. But there are modifications even here. In Rites A and B for Holy Communion of the Alternative Service Book of the Church of England the 'Summary of the Law', given in the Gospels, appears as a legitimate alternative to the Decalogue. And the Methodist Service Book in the rubrics for the Order of Holy

Communion simply indicates that it is appropriate to say the Ten
Commandments on one Sunday or another in Advent and Lent. It
is not known how often they *are* said in these two churches – perhaps
not very often. And it is highly unlikely that any church members
will ever again be brought before a church court for not honouring
their parents.

But as a statement of the *moral* law the Decalogue still largely
holds its ground in Britain and the other Western countries. This is
not to say that it is universally obeyed (that would be a laughable
suggestion), or indeed that it is obeyed nearly as often as in previous
periods of Christian civilization. It is to say that when people break
any of the Ten Commandments, most of them have a sense of guilt,
profound or not so profound, and usually embark on a long process
of self-justification, or, if that cannot be managed, of justification in
the eyes of their friends – in the form of 'I wasn't *really* stealing', or
'I couldn't help myself', or (more subtly) 'the situation was such that
adultery was the more moral alternative'. So long as it is borne in
mind that the veto on murder has nothing to do with actions per-
formed in the defence of one's country, but only with private homi-
cide, it can safely be said that this and the other nine Commandments
still serve as the external and internal conscience of Western
civilization.

This then is a short history of the Decalogue's influence on human
life up to now.

But for the last half century and longer it has been under powerful attack from many quarters, and many people are quite sure that
the attacks are about to succeed. If they do, what a great comfort
it will be to many modern people, who can then relieve their
consciences by forgetting about the Ten Commandments! But is
life as simple as that?

3 *Do they still stand up?*

The first attack on the Commandments comes from those who dismiss them as irrelevant to our times. Their case can be stated in this way, as it refers to the Commandments in turn:

'Not many of those who believe in God are likely nowadays to believe in more than one god; and the moral condemnation of people who do want to believe in several gods smacks of religious intolerance. If anyone wants to make a graven image of his god or goddess, and worship it, why shouldn't he? It's not very likely that anyone today tries to use the name of God (the Devil, perhaps, but not God) for magical purposes (which is probably what the Third Commandment is against), and it would not do much harm if people did attempt that hopeless enterprise. It's impossible to insist as a moral duty that no one should do any work on Sunday in our complicated society (machines have to be kept going, trains have to be kept running, and parsons, parents, milkmaids and shepherds have always had to be exempted from this regulation). Theft, murder and perjury, no doubt, must be checked by the threat of punishment, but adultery and coveting other people's property must be left to the conscience of individuals, not denounced as if they were breaches of a universal moral law. If there *is* a moral law which applies to everyone, the Decalogue does not fill the bill, though it may have done so in the past.'

There is much force in this argument. The Ten Commandments were produced for the benefit of a nomadic people, and their value was still recognized when that people became agricultural and gradually urban. They still managed to keep their force during the development of Graeco-Roman civilization, with a good deal of help from Roman law. But once capitalism, industrialism and technology took over, they quickly ceased to apply to any but a very few of the situations in which modern men and women find themselves. There is no condemnation to be found among them of the 'civilized' sins of blackmail, fraud, breach of contract, insider dealing, promiscuity, drug-dealing, child abuse, slavery, or the exploitation of persons, races and sexes, nor is any account taken of the ruthless pursuit of power and wealth which is endemic in modern society.

There is no answer to these objections if we take the Commandments literally, or suppose that they cover the whole range of moral choices. But if we do not take them literally, then we can properly consider whether, in spite of their extreme antiquity, they embody principles which apply to situations far exceeding in number and complexity the specific actions which they approve or condemn. And this, surely, is what they have been widely held to do in a whole succession of human societies which have differed more and more widely from their original setting.

On these lines, we can suggest (and will do so more fully later in this book) that obsession with the 'false gods' of power, pleasure and sex deserves moral condemnation, and that inordinate devotion to material objects such as wealth and property certainly comes within the scope of moral judgment. We can suggest, also, that the family, even in a modern setting, involves a whole pattern of moral obligations, and that coveting the property of others (though few people any longer regard a wife as property, which is what the Decalogue does) has not become less ethically wrong by being actively encouraged in many departments of modern society, by certain aspects of Government policy and by a constant barrage of advertisements.

Looked at in this way the Ten Commandments properly interpreted still have a claim to be a reasonably full statement of the moral law. There is no doubt that the world would be a happier place, and social justice would be more actual and more clearly visible, if all their prescriptions were carried out by everybody.

A second attack on the divine authority (even divine dictation) claimed for the Decalogue, and on its religious sanctions, is launched on philosophical grounds, and we must discuss philosophy for the next few pages. This attack comes first from those who do not believe in the existence of God, naturally enough; it would be surprising if it did not, although in fact some cynics among the atheists do not raise this objection, as they think that belief in the God whom they do not personally believe to exist is a useful incentive to good behaviour among less enlightened persons than themselves.

But it is not only atheists who mount this attack. There are some Christian teachers who strongly object to the invocation of divine authority. The existence and nature of God (they say), which are factual, have nothing to do with questions of right and wrong, which are moral; and the factual world and the moral world are distinct from each other. Logically, and with the proper use of language, you cannot argue, they say, from what is to what ought to be; you cannot argue from a fact to a duty.

These statements will be so surprising to many people that they need further explanation. It is argued thus: the earth revolves on its own axis and travels round the sun a certain number of times in the course of that period which we call a year. These are facts; nothing whatever in the way of a duty or a moral judgment follows from these facts. You cannot logically say: 'the earth travels round the sun, and therefore people ought to study astronomy, or wear warm clothes at certain times of that journey'. They may study astronomy, or wear suitable clothes in cold weather, but the facts of the weather do not impose on them a duty to do so, and they are not morally better if they do these things. If you look carefully at the language which we use about facts and the different language that we use about duties, you will see, it is said, that this must be so.

This applies no less to the supreme fact, God, it is claimed. No duty follows from it – in the form of worship, love, the good life or anything at all. God is, and that's an end to it. The existence of God imposes on me no duty at all.

Then again, it is argued, if we do good things or perform our duty, because God has commanded us to do so, we are not acting as free moral beings; we are just submitting to a law outside ourselves. 'The truly moral person acts freely in accordance with his or her own inner principles, not at the behest of another, even God. After all, if we believe that God has prescribed a certain course of action, it is prudent to follow it, since we do not know, or perhaps we think we do know, the consequences of not following it. But this is not real morality and our actions are not good at all – merely sensible. Morality must be autonomous, self-regulating, free from all connection with God, to be worthy of its name.'

This double argument, based on certain logical principles, deserves consideration more careful than Christians are inclined to give it. Christians should not try to escape from logic. If a traditional or habitual way of thinking is seen to be illogical, then it must be abandoned, or at least severely questioned. That is true even though we know that there are many other ways of finding truth as well as logic. Moreover, from another point of view Christians are surely concerned to see that such goodness and love as they can attain are not imposed from above or outside, but are freely and personally chosen.

Now it is certainly true that a large number of facts have no moral implications whatever. No duty is laid on me by the facts that the earth goes round the sun, that William of Normandy invaded this island in 1066, that Hitler planned to exterminate the Jews and to conquer the world, that Mount Everest is about 29,000 feet high (though mountaineers have been heard to say that the only reason why they climb that mountain is that it is *there*). These facts may shock or surprise me, or merely interest me. If I decide to do something about them, it is not the facts that lay an obligation on me, but my own moral ideas about justice and truth. So much must be conceded. But with God the case is surely different. He is a different kind of fact from every other fact. He is the sovereign of the universe, and has a perfect right to order me, and the rest of humankind, to do certain things and refrain from doing certain other things, and to indicate to me what these things are. He is also loving, caring and compassionate; and he has given me the freedom to choose his way or not. He exercises his right to command by not coercing me; and then he arouses my sense of gratitude and of duty, often indicates the consequences of this or that action, and leaves me free to make his will my will if I so choose, to co-operate with his purposes, or not.

Admittedly this was not the idea of God with which Moses and many Christians in the past were working. They thought of God as all-just, and taught that his justice was tinged with mercy; but in the end they asserted of him the willingness to punish and even to destroy those who were recalcitrant. But we in our time must assert that the truly Christian view of him is different. On *this* view we can still claim a divine origin for the morality enshrined in the Ten Commandments, while acknowledging their limitations, and admitting that wrong sanctions have often been imposed.

But now let us consider the position in which we should find ourselves if we concluded that the Ten Commandments, and all such moral instruction, entirely lacked divine authority. We should then have concluded that morality stands on its own. Many people do indeed live moral lives without any belief in divine authority. They claim to know within themselves, or by reference to some ideal for humanity which they have embraced, how life should be lived, and live it that way themselves, no doubt because they are fundamentally decent people.

But there is a grave difficulty about this. Even if my moral perceptions tell me what is right and what is wrong, why should I choose what is right and reject what is wrong, if I do not want to?

The most popular answer is 'utilitarianism' – the view that 'right' is what promotes the greatest good of the greatest number, and that this is our best guide for life. 'Promoting the greatest good of the greatest number' is indeed a good working definition of what is right; there are, and will be, interminable arguments as to what constitutes this 'greatest good', but it is now quite generally agreed that the furtherance of justice, peace, freedom from poverty and freedom of thought, speech and religion for as many people as possible is included in it. This is indeed a splendid foundation on which to build one's life. But it gives us no answer to the nagging questions which have always discredited utilitarianism: what actually makes it my duty to promote 'the greatest good of the greatest number'? I may even be prepared to assert that 'the greatest good of the greatest number' is an idea thought up in envy by the weak in order to counter the activities of the smaller number of the strong. On what grounds, in that case, can I be blamed if I seek my own good and let everyone else fall into ruin? I shall be thoroughly hated, no doubt, if I do this, but no moral disgrace attaches to me.

Plato grasped this point a very long time ago, and showed in *The Republic* that it is very hard to refute the strong and clever man who seizes as much power and wealth as he possibly can. Such a man if he is wise will make sure that his deceits and acts of violence go un-detected, and be careful to gain a reputation for benevolence by doing some good to his fellow human beings on his way up to the top. Plato in the end concludes that the villain is impregnable unless it can be shown that he is acting against the Idea of the Good, the goodness inherent in the universe. Utilitarianism will not confute him. If certain newspaper tycoons, who grab everything that they can get, but in the process give employment to thousands of people, spring to mind at this point – well and good.

Belief in an absolute standard of morality has been out of favour for some time among philosophers and moral theologians, but it begins to seem that no valid moral judgments are possible without it. If so, it has to be an absolute standard which is not created by humankind but one that is inherent in the nature of the universe (as Plato thought), in the cosmic order, in ultimate reality, or (as Christians, Jews and Muslims say) in God.

It has still to be asked, of course, how we are to identify this absolute standard, and find out what it prescribes. Jews find it in the Torah, based on the Ten Commandments; Muslims in the Koran, which also shows the great influence of the Ten Commandments; Christians in the life and teachings of Jesus Christ, who held the Ten Commandments in great respect. So the Ten Commandments are once again in the picture!

This is not to say that those who deny that there is or can be an absolute standard of morality are bound to live immoral lives. Of course not. They may well, and many of them do, live lives whose goodness is equal or superior to that of religious people. Such people have moral standards of their own (often, in modern jargon, called 'values'), and live up to them nobly, often more nobly than Christians live up to theirs. But it is to say that the reasoning with which they support their ethical position is faulty.

But we still have to take account of a rearguard attack launched by many non-Christians, and some Christians, on all moral systems of any sort whatever (including, of course, the Decalogue), whether they claim to have divine sanction or not. These teachers point out that moral systems differ so much from one another, according to the age or culture or nature or class where they originate, that it is irrational to claim that there is one overriding moral system of which the existing systems are imperfect examples. Moreover, they say, the human situation changes from age to age, from year to year and even from minute to minute, and the speed of change is for ever increasing in our time; any moral rule which is relevant to one age or one situation is put out-of-date by the next. We have to respond to our situations, not to those of the past, and the old rules are of no value to us.

So what? On this argument, we have to deal with every contingency and every choice, as they arise, by the aid of our own moral perception, our own insight, our own intuition. We may well consult others when we have to make a decision, we may even take a look at past codes of conduct, just in case they may throw some light on the present; but in the end the choice is ours and ours alone, unhampered by precept or precedent. We have no option, in other words, but a 'situation ethic'.

Now, it cannot be denied that moral systems differ from one another, and frequently conflict and collide. In fact, it may be that the only moral precept which is common to all systems is the veto on murder committed for financial gain. But the fact that in ordinary life and in the courts there is lively disagreement among the witnesses to a particular event does not show that the event did not take place at all; and the disagreement of people and nations and cultures on moral issues by no means shows that there are no moral principles at all – only that there are understandable disputes about what they are. Although if one travels in the Soviet Union, parts of Africa, or, still more, probably, in Japan, one is conscious that people live according to different standards from one's own, and discussion about their merits is difficult: yet, unexpectedly, the history of civilization, in which all continents now share, reveals a gradual convergence and a growing consensus on certain issues, such as the rightness of freedom, peace and justice (even while all nations readily find excuses for not actually promoting them).

Moral intuitions and perceptions are not to be disparaged. Everyone, presumably, has some of these, and those of people with more than average wisdom often point the way forward to a fuller understanding of goodness. But, like moral systems, they often disagree with one another; one person's insight is self-deceit in the eyes of another. There are certainly 'disclosure situations', in the famous phrase of I. T. Ramsey – situations in which it becomes luminously clear that *this*, and nothing else, is the thing to do. But they are rare, and there are large tracts of ordinary life where the choices to be made are not between black and white, but between two or more shades of grey, and no sudden 'disclosure' comes to our rescue. So 'situation ethics' does not really cope with the actual circumstances of life.

Thus there is still a strong case for believing that an absolute standard of morality exists, that it has divine authority and a theological basis, and that it is at least partially – but no doubt only partially – revealed in many of the Ten Commandments.

But Christians, with the New Testament open in front of them or in their minds, will not be satisfied with that. For them the Ten Commandments are very useful, but they have been taught in the Gospels that they are not enough. 'Unless your righteousness exceeds the righteousness of the Scribes and Pharisees, you cannot enter the Kingdom of heaven' (Matt. 5.20).

4 *The Commandments transformed*

In the contemporary discussions of the nature of God, the person of Christ, the Virgin Birth, the Resurrection, Christian unity, the ordination of women, and all the other subjects which make the Christian scene exceptionally lively, it is easy to forget that the basic concern of Jesus – whose teaching is, or should be, after all, at the heart of every discussion – was the Kingdom of God. Everything he said and did was immediately related to it; his whole purpose on earth was to preach it, invite people into it and to embody it in his own words and actions, and in his life and death. Yet it is possible to read whole treatises of modern theology, or elaborate expositions of Christian ethics, without coming across any mention of it, or any mention which is more than casual and incidental. This is plainly shocking.

To make matters worse, the phrase itself is frequently used as a mere cliché; or, more frequently still, it is seriously misunderstood in the interests of some particular point of view. At one time the most common mistake was to equate it with the church, which is certainly not the Kingdom, but the agent of the Kingdom, and sometimes very inadequate in that capacity. So the church has sometimes asserted its right to speak as God on earth. The originator of this particular mistake was probably Augustine of Hippo. In his treatise on the *City of God* he made a striking and valid distinction between 'the kingdom of this world' and 'the Kingdom of God', the earthly and the heavenly cities, with two different sets of laws; and for the most part he described the church as the representative of the heavenly city, not the city itself. But he sometimes slipped into identifying the two; or at least he was so understood by his followers and successors. This understanding suited the builders of the mediaeval church only too well, and they had no hesitation about making the identification. It could not possibly have been in the mind of Jesus, and it has led to the inordinate and insupportable claims made for the mediaeval church which did much to provoke the Reformation. Augustine has a lot to answer for in this respect, but he is not entirely to blame.

A mistake of a quite different kind was made by Protestants who equated the Kingdom with the society based on peace and justice which they promised for the world. They even thought that they could bring in 'the Kingdom of God'! No doubt many of the ideas which they promoted were consistent with the nature of the Kingdom as Jesus preached it, but he certainly had no particular social programme or shape of human society in mind; and it is not for us to bring in the Kingdom.

When the church was eventually seen to be very different from the Kingdom, and the hopes of social gospellers were dashed by wars and the continuance of gross injustice, many people swung over to another error, and asserted that the Kingdom was an inward reality in the soul. They seized on a mistranslation of Jesus' words 'the Kingdom of God is among you', rendered in the Authorized Version as 'the Kingdom of God is within you'. But the description is in palpable conflict with the reply of Jesus to the question of John the Baptist, when he said that the presence of the Kingdom was manifested by the healing of the sick and the preaching of the Good News to the poor.

We must try to put the record straight.

The Kingdom of God is better called 'the kingly rule of God, or better still, 'the royal rule of God (lest the heresy that God always acts in a masculine manner – that of a king, and not a queen – is further perpetuated), or perhaps even better still 'the sovereignty of God'. The Kingdom of God (if we must still, as probably we must, use the familiar phrase) is present wherever the sovereign rule of God is accepted and obeyed in the life of an individual, a group, a church, a nation, or the world. It is present in all such circumstances, but not of course in its fullness; its final fulfilment is in the future, when God's will is done on earth as it is already done in heaven. The Kingdom has come in Jesus, it comes whenever God's will is done, it will come fully when God's will is perfectly done.

It is in the context of Jesus' emphatic teaching on the Kingdom of God, and only in that context, that his familiar sayings about the way to live can be properly understood:

'Love the Lord your God with all your heart, with all your soul, with all your mind. That is the greatest commandment. It comes first. The second is like it: love your neighbour as yourself. Everything in the Law and the prophets hangs on these two commandments' (Matt. 22.37–40).

'You have learned that our forefathers were told, "Do not commit murder; anyone who commits murder must be brought to judgment." But what I tell you is this: Anyone who nurses anger against his brother must be brought to judgment . . .'

'You have learned that they were told, "Do not commit adultery." But what I tell you is this: If a man looks on a woman with a lustful eye, he has already committed adultery with her in his heart . . .'

'Again you have learned that our forefathers were told "Do not break your oath," and "Oaths sworn to the Lord must be kept." But what I tell you is this: You are not to swear at all. Plain "Yes" or "No" is all you need to say . . .'

'You have learned that they were told, "Eye for eye, tooth for tooth". But what I tell you is this: Do not set yourself against the man who wrongs you. If someone slaps you on the right cheek, turn and offer him your left . . .'

'You have learned that they were told, "Love your neighbour, hate your enemy." But what I tell you is this: Love your enemies and pray for your persecutors; only so can you be children of your heavenly Father . . .' (Matt. 5.21–45).

'I give you a new commandment: love one another; as I have loved you, so you are to love one another' (John 13.34).

'If you love me, you will obey my commands' (John 14.25).

In all these sentences, except the last two, we can be confident that we hear, as nearly as possible, the actual words of Jesus. In the last two the author of the Fourth Gospel, after many years' reflection, has crystallized the authentic teaching of Jesus in a few very well-chosen words.

These pronouncements of Jesus (which will be fully discussed in later chapters) are not addressed to the world at large; they are addressed to those who have accepted his invitation to enter the Kingdom of God. Others, including people of many religions, have listened to them and tried bravely to obey them, and they have not by any means entirely failed. To many other people they seem beautiful but impossibly idealistic. But the thing to remember is that they are addressed to the citizens of the Kingdom of God; they are not intended to give advice to the world in general. They are the 'laws' (though this word needs explanation) of the Kingdom of God.

As such they cast an entirely fresh light on the Jewish Law, including the Ten Commandments, and on much else. Both of the two 'Great Commandments' are to be found, separately, in the Old Testament (Deut. 6.5 and Lev. 19.18), and some of the rabbis in the time of Jesus had gone some way towards linking them together as a summary of the Law. This is shown by the story in Luke 10.25–28, where a teacher of the Law answers Jesus by enunciating them together. Jesus allied himself with these rabbis, but he went further than they did: he went, in fact, to the limit, so that the Great Commandments become not a summary, but a re-statement of the Law.

Jesus' attitude to the Law sometimes seems confusing and contradictory. At one point he says that 'so long as heaven and earth endure, not a letter, not a stroke will disappear from the Law until all that must happen has happened' (or 'before all it stands for is achieved') (Matt. 5.18); at others he corrects the Law out of hand, as in the six sentences from the Sermon on the Mount just quoted above. Was he for the Law, or against it? The truth is that he first approves the Law, and then re-states it in the two Great Commandments; and in the course of re-stating it he transforms it. The Ten Commandments contain virtually no mention of love; but love is the very basis of the Great Commandments. We are commanded to love God and our neighbour. But this, on the face of it, is absurd. Love cannot be commanded, and anyone who tries to command it is surely crying for the moon – like parents who order their children to make friends with so and so, on the ground that he or she is a suitable companion for them; and this, we know, does not work.

So what is Jesus about? He is saying that if we belong to the Kingdom of God, truly and sincerely, we *shall* love God and our neighbour. Of course, we have to be reminded that this is so, and urged to carry out the implications of our membership of God's Kingdom. But the 'commandment' to love is not a prescription (loving by order is not love at all, anyway), but an indication of what happens when we enter God's Kingdom. We are changed inwardly by our acceptance of God's royal rule; we begin to do what we had previously thought impossible, even to the inconceivable extent of loving our enemies.

The Great Commandments are indeed the 'laws of the kingdom'; but the word law is now used in a very different sense from the usual one; it is used in much the same way as we use it when we talk of the law of gravity, which does not command objects to fall, but describes the way in which they do fall.

From re-statement, Jesus goes on to reinterpretation. In this the keeping of the Law becomes primarily a matter for the man or woman 'within'. Love for God and one's neighbour is normally shown by certain outward acts; by worship and neighbourly deeds; if it is not, the suspicion arises that it is not real, but only professed – that we are humbugs. But this is only the first test. The nub of the matter is what is happening inside us, for this is where love (or its opposite) resides. If I do not love God within myself, all my attendances at worship, and even my reception of the sacraments, are nugatory. If I do not love my neighbour inside myself as deeply as I love myself (and *that* love is very deep), all my 'neighbourly' acts will be cold and uncompassionate (and probably seen to be such by the intended beneficiary).

The lasting effect on my life of my love for God and neighbour becomes 'inward' too. As Jesus points out (Matt. 6.5), real prayer to God is in 'the secret place'; the words of it are no doubt often, of necessity, audible and public, but the reality is within, and it is this inward reality that makes the words sincere and genuine. To take extreme cases, as Jesus did, my neighbour-love is negated by the nursing of anger against another as much as by actually murdering him or her. So with adultery; lust may not proceed to the act of adultery, but it is lust just the same – the absolute negation of neighbour-love.

Jesus' interpretation of the Law does not simply internalize it; it personalizes it also. 'Eye for eye, tooth for tooth' is an abstract, impersonal principle. It is, of course, an improvement on 'the whole body for an eye or tooth', or 'a whole nation for one individual's crime', which the Nazis claimed as a justification for Kristallnacht – the smashing of all the Jewish synagogues – in 1938; but it is still impersonal and abstract. An injury is done; the compensating injury (i.e. imprisonment or a fine) automatically follows. The matter may end there – it sometimes does; but it may do the exact opposite. The offender may nurse a grievance against the courts and the police, and look for the next opportunity to do them harm. Thus another recruit is added to the criminal class, and the war between criminals and police is taken a stage further. That may be the best that even a civilized society can do, but it is a poor best, as we can see in the condition of our own nation at present. In the Kingdom of God we treat each other as persons, even to the length of allowing someone who has assaulted us once to assault us again; for our object is to turn an enemy into a friend, not to continue the feud or exact our pound of flesh. We are to forgive, not seven times, but seventy times seven.

In society at large to love our friends and hate our enemies is regarded as the essence of patriotism, especially in time of war. So we stereotype the Germans, or the Ulster Catholics or Protestants, or the followers of the Ayatollah, and hate the lot, which is easy enough, but simply prolongs the conflict (fortunately hatred is inclined to cool down and disappear, when the war or other emergency is over, except in some revengeful people, and in the no doubt very special case of the Jewish people and the Nazis). But in the Kingdom of God we remember that Germans, and Jews, and Irish people, and Afrikaaners, are persons, and can begin to love them and pray for them as persons, even while we are doing our best to counteract their activities.

So, once we have agreed to love our neighbour as ourselves, we have undertaken to treat him or her as a person, just as we treat ourselves and like to be treated. No longer is he or she just the member of a social class, or a race, or a nation, or a mere statistic on the register of the unemployed, or of the Old Age Pensioners in special need. Loving him or her as a person, we desire for him or her all the good things that we desire for ourselves (and that is probably quite a long list); and we work as hard as we can to provide them.

Moreover, Jesus' reinterpretation of the Law brings the citizens of God's Kingdom out of the jungles of literalism and legalism. We do not need any longer to work out the precise application of every single one of the Ten Commandments, and then lay down a set of invariable laws. Each human situation is different from every other human situation (as we have seen in another connection), and requires a different response; even situations which seem to be the same as others in the past turn out on careful examination to be different in one way or another, as anybody who has tried to give advice in marital or other sexual situations will certainly testify.

Thus we can abolish at a stroke the myriad regulations laid down in the Pentateuch, and in subsequent rabbinical and Christian rulebooks. Life continually bursts the bounds of ethical manuals, and it is absolutely useless to go through the Old and New Testaments in order to find a rule which we can apply in a modern situation. To grasp this we need only to glance at the Levitical laws on the payment of debts, the punishment of slaves, the burning of witches and the stoning of adulteresses. It is absurd to read off the right way to treat homosexuals from the book of Leviticus. Jesus, in the Sermon on the Mount, does not lay down rules for any situation; he gives

us examples of the way in which the universal law of love may work
out in this case or that. The rest is left to us. We have seen that there
is only one law in the Kingdom of God, the law of love; it is for us,
with all the help that we can get from the church, the Bible and our
friends, to find out the way in which this law applies to the actual
situation in which we find ourselves. There is a great deal of the
'higher' Christian commonsense in the writings of Paul (and sometimes, it is to be feared, of the opposite). But he was speaking in the
context of his own times and the needs and questions of the people
to whom he was writing. So he provides no rules and regulations for
us, but only useful guidelines; and his guidelines are all the more
useful because he also asserts the primacy of love, and consciously
applies the principle of love to each situation. This is what we also
have to do for ourselves.

It is in the light of all this that we shall look at each of the Ten
Commandments, asking in each case what significance (if any) it has
for us as part of the universal law, and then going on to look for
its significance as it has been transformed by the teaching of Jesus
about the Kingdom. In the course of this we shall have to justify
and amplify some of what has been adumbrated already.

We need to be aware in advance that the task before us will be
complicated by two factors to which no allusion has yet been made:
1. As Augustine and Luther and Wesley pointed out in their day,
Christians have a double citizenship – we are to live by the laws of
God's royal rule, but we also are subject to the commands of a
society where these laws are only partially acknowledged, when
they are acknowledged at all; 2. although at first sight Jesus teaches
an individualistic morality, this is not really so, and the social and
political implications of his words will certainly come out from time
to time.

These are complications. But there is also a unity which underlies
all that Jesus teaches. We are to live the life which he sets before us,
not out of a sense of duty (admirable though that sometimes is), still
less out of a wish to stand well with our fellows, or to win God's
favour, but simply and solely because God loves us without dis-
crimination and irrespectively of our merits. In the Kingdom we

model our lives on the character and actions of God. We love because he first loved us.

There is a further factor which books on Christian ethics sometimes leave out. Christian virtues and the actions which spring from them do not grow by human effort alone, even in the people who seem to be naturally good, still less in the rest of us. The Holy Spirit is not inactive in any part of God's creation; but he works more effectively in those who co-operate with him in the Kingdom of God. Christian virtues are the fruit of the Spirit. That thought should never be absent from our minds. It is the key to the freedom of the children of God.

But before we go further we must consider the place of conscience in the Christian scheme of things.

5 Conscience and the Commandments

By 'conscience' we usually mean the 'sense' or 'faculty' by which we distinguish right and wrong, are urged to do right and avoid wrong, and are blamed if we do what is wrong or fail to do what is right. As such it is highly honoured by the majority of the human race. A conscientious person, one who habitually obeys his or her conscience, is almost universally regarded as a good person, whereas those who are seen frequently to disobey their consciences are almost universally condemned.

Quite a large number of civilized nations respect conscience even to the extent of allowing people to exercise 'conscientious objections' to fighting in time of war or to preparing for war in time of peace, so long as they undertake tasks which are deemed to serve the national welfare.

Closely linked with 'conscience' is 'duty'. In fact, 'to do one's duty' is by most people regarded as identical with obeying one's conscience, though some people would distinguish the two by saying that one's duty *is* such and such, even if one is not informed of this by one's conscience. But for practical purposes they can be treated as having the same role. As W. S. Gilbert, that sardonic moralist, observes in *Ruddigore*:

> Duty, duty must be done,
> The rule applies to everyone:
> And painful though that duty be,
> To shirk the task were fiddle-de-dee.

(It must remain obscure what 'fiddle-de-dee' exactly is, but it is clearly something unpleasant.) William Wordsworth went so far as to call duty 'stern daughter of the voice of God', and there is no doubt that for many religious people, 'doing the will of God', 'doing one's duty' and 'obeying one's conscience' are synonymous terms.

But there are difficulties about all this. We all know from experience, probably our own, how easy it is to deceive oneself about conscience: what we think we are doing on conscientious grounds sometimes turns out to have been motivated by fear of being discovered doing the opposite, or by the wish to fall in with what one's colleagues are doing – or contrariwise, by the simple wish to be different from other people. Then there are many conflicts of duties. I may, for example, be urged by conscience to give money to two or more charities, but have enough money to give to only one.

More seriously, there are the differences of conscience that arise between those who belong to opposing classes or races or nations. In a war, it is agreed (except by pacifists) to be my duty to kill the nation's enemies; but it is equally the duty of those on the other side to kill me. The whole question of espionage brings up this problem in an acute form. It may be my duty if I am in Russia to spy on its defences in the interests of my own country; but it is equally the duty of the Soviets to imprison me if I am caught doing it.

Most seriously of all, there are the occasions when my duty seems to be overridden by a higher imperative, urging me to do something contrary to what I have always believed to be my duty; if I proceed to do it I am disobeying my conscience. It is my plain duty to support my family and care for my aged parents: but what if I am called to undertake a dangerous task from which I may not return? We need to remember the usually neglected saying of Jesus: 'When you have carried out all your orders, you shall say, "We are servants and deserve no credit; we have only done our duty" ' (Luke 17.10). (In fact, there are singularly few references to duty, and to conscience, in our sense of the word, in the whole New Testament.)

So it seems that conscience is not the supreme court we have usually taken it to be. There may be a higher court still.

We can begin to see our way through this difficulty if we suppose that conscience is not, in fact, a finely tuned instrument for discerning the right course of action in a situation which confronts us; but a repository, a kind of reference book, of past moral judgments which we consult when a new occasion for decision presents itself. These moral judgments, stored up in our conscience, are those which we learned from our parents, or from our education, or from the ethics of our country, class, sex, group or profession, or from the church to which we belong; with the addition of those (if any) which we have ourselves formed as we have gone through life. All, or most, of these may have been sound in the past; indeed, in a way, they embody the wisdom of our culture and of our traditional morality; but they are not necessarily sound in the present time, or truly applicable to our present situation.

To throw 'conscience' and 'duty' overboard for good and all on these grounds would clearly be stupid; but to obey them implicitly on all occasions would certainly be unwise and irresponsible. Our best course is to consult our conscience, and at the same time to inquire whether guidance from any other source is forthcoming. If there is nothing which 'improves on' conscience, then conscience is to be obeyed, and if we obey our consciences we shall certainly not go very far wrong. But if there is an imperative 'beyond the call of duty', then it takes precedence over conscience and duty.

But how do we know when this is so? It is here that the distinction between the Ten Commandments (which are written on our consciences, and stand, in general, for 'duty') and the Commandments of the Lord Jesus (which must take precedence over the Ten Commandments) comes to the rescue, if we are Christians. In other faiths other help is to be found. As we look at each Commandment in turn, we shall see how the demands of conscience are superseded by the higher claims of the Gospel.

6 'You shall have no other god to set beside me'

It is highly unlikely that Moses was a strict monotheist. He did not assert that 'there is no God but Jahweh'. What he did assert, and emphasize in the First Commandment, was that Jahweh, who had enlightened and inspired him when he was working in the employment of his father-in-law Jethro, was the God for the Hebrews to worship and obey; he was to be, for all intents and purposes, their God, who would lead them out of slavery into freedom and make them into a nation. We could say that Moses was a virtual monotheist, since the other gods, the gods of other peoples, counted for nothing in his eyes. No doubt they looked after their own people reasonably well, but Jahweh could do much better for his people, and to set the other gods beside him would be the height of folly and disloyalty (adultery, as the prophets later called it). So Moses, and the Hebrew people under his guidance, were 'henotheists', to use the technical title. It is a quirk of history that the God whom Moses chose for his people (or as we might wish to put it, who chose Israel to be his people) was probably the God of the Midianites, who were to become Israel's bitter enemies (whose hosts, as the old hymn has it, prowl and prowl around).

The original meaning of the First Commandment thus becomes clear; the Hebrews were not to put any other god or any goddess on a par with Jahweh. The importance of this Commandment is also clear. The Hebrews were a mixed and disorganized body of men and women and children – in other words, a mob. They had seen and suffered from the prosperity and power which the gods and goddesses of Egypt had (apparently) allotted to the Egyptian nation. They were now invited to undertake a difficult and dangerous enterprise, launched against the might of Egypt. They needed a unifying factor and a focus of faith and courage if they were to take even the first step. This was what Moses gave them in the form of the worship of Jahweh; and his policy was brilliantly successful.

The Hebrews, however, as we know from their traditional stories, were not by any means totally converted at a stroke from the miscellaneous religions which they had previously followed; and when anything went wrong, and Jahweh did not seem to deliver the goods, they were very much inclined to rebel against the leadership, and slip back into their old ways. But Moses and his successors stood firm and prevailed – at least officially – although there were no doubt many pockets of non-Jahwistic belief and worship; and many people, no doubt, hedged their bets by worshipping both Jahweh, as required, and the local deities as occasion demanded.

The real test of the Commandment came when the Hebrews gradually made the transition from a nomadic to an agricultural existence. Jahweh was God of the desert, with no fixed and statutory place of worship, and thus eminently suitable for a nomadic people. Farming, even of the simplest kind, required knowledge and skills which the Hebrews did not at first possess. When their crops were poor they put the blame (as is human) on the God whom they were ordered to worship, and contrasted his failure with the success of their neighbours, the Canaanites, whose gods and goddesses were known to promote fertility in plants and animals and human beings. Many gods had 'Baal' as their title, but the greatest of them was Hadad, the god of winter storms, who had brought order out of primaeval chaos, and had tamed the waters to provide the moisture for the vegetation which all need for life. There was also the powerful goddess Astarte (she has many names), whose widespread cult employed sacred prostitutes, men and women, offering union with the goddess and the encouragement of procreation. Where these deities ruled, the land seemed to flow with more milk and honey than did the territory of the austere Jahweh. So the stage was set for a contest between the deities of fertility and the God of the desert.

The contest lasted several centuries, and it was only when the eighth-century prophets of Jahweh could point eloquently and convincingly to Jahweh's activities in history, and to the immorality encouraged by the Canaanite deities, that it began to go in Jahweh's favour. The place of Amos, Micah, Isaiah and others in history is that they re-animated the failing loyalty of kings and people to Jahweh, who, they claimed, had brought them out of Egypt and given them nationhood. They did it so effectively that Canaanite deities were finally extruded not only from private and public worship, but from existence altogether. 'The gods of the heathen are idols, made by human hands; Jahweh, the God of Israel, is the God of the whole earth, the only God,' was their triumphant consensus.

So monotheism was the climax of a long process, not a sudden revelation on Mount Sinai, and it finds its classic expression in Deut. 6.4: 'Hear, O Israel; the Lord our God is one Lord.'

From that time in the late seventh century the First Commandment has been understood, in Judaism and far beyond, as insisting on the strict monotheism which is basic to Judaism and Islam. This understanding of it has, of course, been part of the Christian tradition from the time of Jesus himself; and it has remained part of the Western religious consciousness even when the other doctrines of Judaism and Christianity have been discarded.

This religious consciousness has waned perceptibly in recent years, and in the case of atheists seems to have disappeared altogether, though some of them can be caught out praying to or thanking the God whose existence they deny.

But there are many kinds of atheist, and strict atheists are probably not very numerous. These are the people who rule out the possibility of God's existence on rational grounds, and therefore regard all religion as illusion. To them, no doubt, the First Commandment has no relevance. Instead of being asked to obey this, they can legitimately be faced with the questions: 1. If there is no God, how has the universe come together, and how does it stay together? 2 If there is no God, and therefore no universal principle behind the universe, how is knowledge of any sort possible? The only answer given to both these questions is 'by chance'. But chance is not something which exists, but just a convenient word for describing the initiation and operation of forces, and the occurrence of events, in which no underlying pattern can be discerned. So it is no answer at all. Thus the strict atheists are in a very difficult position, and this perhaps is why there are not very many of them.

But the First Commandment is relevant to the other kinds of atheist. Many of them have ceased to believe in God because of a certain mental inertia; they have slipped into non-belief in conformity with the atmosphere of the times, or with the corporate attitude of the groups of people with whom they are associated; or perhaps because of some real or imagined harm done to them by the church or by churchpeople. A conversion to atheism sometimes happens because a personal tragedy has destroyed their belief in the God in which they think that they are asked to believe. They have not worked out the logical implications of belief or of non-belief. Many of them would admit that they have given very little thought to the matter, and if pressed will say that they are probably agnostics rather than atheists.

But this subsidence into non-belief in God has not killed the religious instinct which is said to be in us all. As several writers have put it, there is a God-shaped hole in the hearts of most people, including atheists. Many claimants have come forward to fill that hole.

Some of these 'new' religions are imports from the wisdom of the East, ancient and venerable, and thought to be immune from the materialism which has corrupted European civilization and infected Christianity itself. Zen Buddhism and 'transcendental meditation' are clear examples of this, with the advantage for modern men and women that you can engage in them without deciding whether God exists or not.

The relentless pursuit of wealth and of power through wealth has always been the unacknowledged religion of many in society, and this has reached a new climax today. Some of the other religions are revivals of ancient cults which Christians had fondly thought to have been finally eliminated by the advance of Christianity. The cult of sex reaches right back into the early days of human society; we have just seen it in the religion of the ancient Canaanites; it was powerful enough in the form of the worship of Aphrodite (Venus) in Corinth to be a dangerous rival to the Christian gospel as preached by Paul; it has reappeared, sometimes under a Christian guise, in various parts of Europe through the centuries. In Western Europe and America it has now reached one of the many peak-times of its history, taking both the semi-mystical form advocated by D. H. Lawrence, who saw it as the key to the problems of the universe, and the cruder form encouraged and exploited by *The Sun* and *The News of the World*, which take it for granted that the satisfaction of sexual desire (often mingled with the lust for power) is the chief purpose of human existence and the highest happiness of men and women (while hypocritically pretending to disapprove of those who live accordingly).

Belief in astrology is also a revival of ancient beliefs. In the pre-astronomical age there were good arguments for the view that the heavenly bodies influenced or even controlled human affairs, and the signs of the Zodiac could be held to reveal the pattern of that influence or control. This view is no longer scientifically tenable, since no astral effect on human character or actions has ever been demonstrated, and people born under the same sign plainly exhibit very different characteristics and have very different experiences. Yet the belief in 'what the stars foretell' has revived in recent times, and many people, presumably, plan their lives with the astrological predictions in mind with which the newspapers provide them.

Others believe in chance; others, desperately, in fate. But the most potent and the most widely worshipped substitute for the God of the Bible is the nation state. Utter devotion to one's country, or tribe, goes back far beyond the origins of the great religions of the world. It has often formed uneasy alliances with all of them, not least with Christianity. In our century, it has tended to be dormant during ordinary times; but it erupted strongly in Nazi Germany, and does so in every country in time of war. Those who thought that it had declined in this country were rudely awakened by the chauvinism which was aroused by the Falklands War. It is, of course, an essentially illogical religion, since its devotees in every country believe in their own nation, right or wrong, and most of all when nations are in conflict with one another. Both belligerents cannot have God on their side! Yet the illogicality does not stand in the way of absolute loyalty to one's country. Cecil Spring-Rice's words

> I vow to thee, my country, all earthly things above,
> Entire and whole and perfect, the service of my love;
> The love that asks no questions, the love that stands the test,
> That lays upon the altar the dearest and the best,

express the religious feeling of most English people during the First World War, and still do in many cases today.

These God-substitutes have an almost common characteristic. In spite of the grandiose language which some of them use, and the literature which especially the cult of sex has created, they have all fallen short, except in one case, of commanding the total self-oblation of individuals which the great world religions have inspired. No one has died a martyr to Venus, or to astrology, or to ambition, or to the pursuit of wealth. For the most part these deities jostle one another as rivals in the pantheon. The one exception is patriotism, which certainly has its martyrs, though we should not characterize all who have died for their country in this way.

All these so-called atheists are descending into polytheism; and they, like Christians who mingle their faith with the pursuit of wealth, or even astrology, need to be faced with the First Commandment. European civilization in its long search for truth arrived at monotheism through Judaism and Christianity; not, indeed, immediately. Often the entry of Christianity soon captured the minds of the educated few, but took a very long time to penetrate the deepest thoughts of all Europeans. It eventually did so, and the completion of this process at the end of the Middle Ages was the signal for the real advance of philosophy, theology and the sciences, though the Schoolmen had already shown the way forward. If we now regress to the worship of many gods and goddesses, each taking care of one

compartment of human life, we risk the disintegration of our thinking, and in the end the disintegration of civilized society. Perhaps
this disintegration has already begun. We need to be pulled up short
by the stark choice which faces us – God or nothing. Polytheism is
not a third option.

So much for the modern application of the Commandment to
society at large. For the Christian, when it is interpreted in the light
of the Gospel, it acquires a more profound significance.

'Love the Lord your God with all your heart, with all your soul,
with all your mind.' We have passed from the negative to the positive, from the exclusion of false objects of worship to the concentra-
tion of the whole personality on the one true object of worship. The
Jewish people had already made that transition as they obeyed the
injunction of Deut. 6; Jesus confirmed it and reinforced it. In due
course Islam did the same in its own way. This indeed is the point
on which Jews, Christians and Muslims are agreed, and from which
they can advance to a greater understanding of one another.

If we love God with our whole person, it follows that we worship him with all our powers. A purely emotional worship, a purely
intellectual worship, a worship which is a matter of willpower only
(a grim determination to do his will) – all of these are inadequate
responses to the majesty of God. Only a total engagement can possibly fill the bill. (Jews and Muslims describe this in terms of their
own spirituality, which includes in each case gratitude and trust and
loyalty and endurance.)

Jesus added a further dimension to the love which God calls
forth. He spoke of the God whose Kingdom he embodied and pro-
claimed as one who loves all his creatures without distinction
between the good and the evil, who loves them without their
deserving his love, who goes out of his way to find them when they
have gone astray, who combines in his person the highest qualities
of fatherhood and motherhood to an infinite degree. The love
which he calls forth from us is no longer compounded just of
reverence and awe, but also of tenderness and of intimacy, without
any quest for a reward:

Not with the hope of gaining aught,
Not seeking a reward;
But as thyself hast lovèd me
O ever-loving Lord!

7 'You shall not make a carved image for yourself'

This is amplified in Ex. 20 into a sweeping condemnation of any image in wood or stone of any shape, human or non-human, or of any natural object in the air, on the land or in the sea. Still less is any Israelite to bow down to or worship any image of any kind wherever found.

As we can see, we cannot easily ascribe this vast prohibition to Moses, since for a long time after him various images used in religious worship were officially tolerated. Gideon, for instance, the great champion of Jahweh, much praised in the Bible, as well as having a harem and seventy sons, set up an 'ephod' (no one quite knows what this was, though it was clearly some kind of image) for the purpose of divining the future. The 'teraphim', images of household gods, were used by the early kings, also for divining the future (always a matter of concern for those in government but not usually available). Jeroboam, the rebel king who seized more than half of Solomon's kingdom at that monarch's death, set up bull images of Jahweh in Samaria, and, although this action was strongly condemned later, he seems at first to have escaped the censure of those of Jahweh's priests who attached themselves to him.

But from an early date it became a basic conviction of the single-minded followers of Jahweh that he was spiritual and invisible and intangible (though not always inaudible), possessing no shape or form, and incapable of being represented by any image whatever.

As this conviction gradually prevailed against the worship of the Canaanitish gods and goddesses of fertility, who could be all too easily portrayed in images which the prophets thought disgusting, so distaste for all images steadily grew until the veto which we know as the Second Commandment became part of the Torah, and was given Mosaic authority.

In view of this it is surprising that in the Temple of Solomon there was probably an image of a brazen serpent, and that in the Holy of Holies were the cherubim, not, of course, chubby angels, as depicted in Renaissance art, but huge sphinxes, or lions with human heads, guarding the throne of Jahweh, and assisted by the winged seraphim, also animal figures with a partly human shape. Surely this was a flouting of the Second Commandment, accepted by Isaiah the prophet without question as the context of his heavenly vision (Isa. 6.1–9)? The answer to be given to this must be found in the second part of the Commandment. 'You shall not bow down to them (the images) or worship them.' The purpose of their presence was officially to draw attention to the glory of Jahweh, and not to attract any veneration to themselves. But, even so, it cannot be denied that they were carved images!

There was no image of Jahweh himself in the Temple of Solomon, or in the Second Temple, built, without the cherubim and seraphim, by exiles returned from Babylon in the sixth century BC; nor was there one in the Temple built by Herod the Great in the first century BC. When Roman power overshadowed the Middle East in the first century BC, the Roman general and notable statesman, Pompey the Great, then engaged in tidying up Armenia and Syria, was invited to intervene in a dispute between two rivals for the Jerusalem High Priesthood (which virtually involved the position of king). He did so very readily – and seized the chance to annex the whole country of Judaea, which thus became a Roman vassal. Pompey entered the ruined city of Jerusalem with his army, and passed through the Temple precincts to the Holy of Holies – an act of terrible sacrilege, because only the High Priest was allowed to enter, and he only on the Day of Atonement. Pompey, careless of such things, observed with amazement that there was no image of God to be seen. For that reason, or for reasons of state, he left the entire Temple intact. Herod the Great, whom the Romans later installed as a puppet king, tried to ingratiate himself with the Jews by rebuilding the Temple in more splendid style than it then possessed, but he had no real understanding of Jewish sensibilities. Not long before the birth of Jesus he put up a golden eagle above the gateway of the Temple, as a symbol of Roman sovereignty. This was an outrage. While Herod lay on his deathbed a little later on, two Pharisees tore the eagle down, and so reasserted the Second Commandment. Herod ordered their summary execution.

In the time of Christ, then, the Second Commandment was passionately observed in Judaism, as it had been already for several centuries. It was taken as binding by the earliest Christians. (There is no mention of Christian images in the New Testament.) It was adopted, with added seriousness, and even ferocity, by Islam at its inception, and occupies a prominent place in the Koran.

But once the Gospel had well and truly penetrated the Gentile world, it was no longer possible to suppress the urge to embody the faith in artistic ways. The second-century pictures in the Roman Catacombs are symbolic, not realistic; Christ is shown as a shepherd, looking rather like a young Greek, or represented by the picture of a fish. Gradually, under Eastern influences, a greater realism appeared. Then after Christianity had been legalized by the Emperor Constantine, the pictures became triumphant and elaborate; first Christ, and later the Blessed Virgin Mary, the angels and the saints, were crowned with haloes in blue, gold, yellow and rainbow colours. Statues also, of Christ, Mary and the saints were placed in churches and at wayside altars, attracting the devotion of the faithful, and often designed to teach some aspect of the faith.

How was this squared with the Second Commandment? Not, perhaps, very convincingly, but in a way which satisfied priests, bishops and people alike. The old veto, it was said, was on representation of the *divine* beings (actually it was wider than that); Christ Incarnate, Mary his mother, and the saints were human (and the angels were semi-human, perhaps), and surely there could be no objection to making images of human beings! The real justification lay partly in the desire to create something beautiful in the service of God, and partly in the need to make it easier for ordinary people to believe in the unseen world and its inhabitants.

After the time of Constantine, the Roman world steadily lost the unity of which it had boasted for so long. Usually there were two co-emperors, one enthroned in Rome and one in Constantinople. The dividing line, often obscure and fought over, was roughly up the Adriatic Sea and into the territory above it. Sometimes the Eastern Emperors claimed lordship over the West as well; sometimes the Western Empire claimed a rather precarious authority for itself. The Eastern Empire was at first much more securely in control of its territory, though in the course of time that territory was steadily eroded by the advance of Islam. The Western Empire was already in the fifth century under attack from the migrating tribes coming down from the north, and many areas sank gradually back into pre-Roman confusion and ignorance, with the Christian church and its bishops as the only civilizing force that was left.

Under these circumstances East and West developed distinct types of spirituality, each claiming to be the true Christian one, and resenting the claims of the other. Complete schism came in the eleventh century, but its roots lay deep in the long history of this theological and liturgical conflict, frequently coming out into the open in the form of disputes about the authority of the Bishop of Rome when he claimed universal suzerainty.

The differences between East and West showed themselves not least in the matter of images. In the West little limitation was placed on the creation and devotional use of both sacred images and sacred pictures. In the East the Second Commandment was still mandatory; but it was generally held that the Commandment did not forbid the use of icons, which are pictures, usually flat, but sometimes in bas relief, painted on wood, or wrought in ivory and other materials. They represented Christ, Mary, or one or other of the saints. Devotion was paid to them in the form of kneeling, kissing and the burning of incense, and they were believed to be capable of working miracles.

But suddenly, in 726, the Eastern Emperor, Leo III, set the whole

Christian world by the ears by ordering the destruction of all images and icons throughout his Empire. His official reason, which can well be defended, and was based on the Second Commandment, was that Christian peasants and priests in the Balkans, ravaged by Arabic invasions, had descended into the superstitious worship of images and icons, and must be recalled to true Christianity. His practical reason was that the Caliph of Bagdad had just ordered the destruction of images throughout Islam, and the Christian Emperor must surely not be outdone in the promotion of spiritual worship. The Emperor was supported by the military, and by some theologians – the military because many of the monks, who favoured the icons, had escaped from military service by entering a monastery at a time when the Empire needed every available man to fight the Muslims.

Leo dismissed and replaced the Patriarch of Constantinople who opposed him, and tried to impose his iconoclasm (the 'smashing of images') on the church in the West. In this latter attempt he failed against the opposition of the Pope, and the Western church was relatively unaffected by the issue and unscathed by the violence which it caused. But in the East there were riots and repression over many years, with occasional interludes under more moderate emperors than Leo. More than a century of bitter controversy had passed before the widespread devotion to icons finally triumphed and the last iconoclastic Emperor died. In 843 a great thanksgiving ceremony was held in Constantinople to give honour to the icons, and it is still celebrated every year as the 'Feast of Orthodoxy' in the Eastern churches.

It was laid down at the Second Council of Nicaea in 787 that icons are to be 'venerated', with a 'relative' love, and God alone is to be 'worshipped', with 'absolute' devotion. Since those times Orthodox Christians in great number have found in their icons, both in church and at home, a focus for their devotions, concentrating their minds on the reality behind and beyond the icons. They have felt themselves to be in the very presence of the Saviour, the Blessed Virgin, or one of the saints. The most famous of all icons is the 'icon of the Trinity', in itself a great work of art, by Rublev, a Russian monk of the fifteenth century. It depicts the three guests who were entertained by Abraham under the terebinth trees of Mamre (Gen. 18.1–8), and in a mysterious way draws the mind towards the love which binds together the Father, the Son and the Holy Spirit. (It is now in a Moscow museum.)

Echoes of the Iconoclastic Controversy gradually died away in the East; in the Western church they were revived at the time of the Reformation. The Reformers saw in the ubiquitous veneration of images, icons and relics, together with pilgrimages and indulgences, a blatant denial of the New Testament teaching that we are saved by grace alone. Many of them set about the elimination of all sacred statues and pictures from the churches which came under their influence, though Martin Luther himself was not nearly so ruthless. (He retained the crucifix in the churches which he sought to renew by the preaching of the Word and the transformation of the Mass.)

The Puritan reformers in England followed the strict Calvinist iconoclastic tradition, and the stripping of the churches for the sake of eliminating idolatry has left an indelible mark on English folk memory.

Not too soon, Christians of all schools of thought have now come to see that both sides in this long and destructive dispute were right and wrong, though they themselves tend, no doubt, in one direction or the other. Those who affirm the veneration of icons and images rightly say that the incarnation of the Son of God establishes the use of images as the vehicles of God's grace. This is what bread and wine are in the eucharist. But to invest them with supernatural powers predisposes untutored people to superstition. Those who reject images and icons are right in insisting that Christian worship must be spiritual, and that it can be corrupted by the misuse of material things. But they sometimes forget the old adage of the Schoolmen: the misuse of something does not remove its proper use.

The conclusion for modern Christians must be that the Second Commandment as it stands has outlived its usefulness as an element in the moral consciousness of the human race, though Jews and Muslims may not agree. Since material things can be sacramental, there is no veto on the painting of pictures and the sculpting of statues as aids to devotion (though the garish and the sentimental should surely, on religious as well as aesthetic grounds, at all costs be avoided). Besides, it is not likely that anyone now will be disposed to bow down and worship the results of human creativity.

But this does not dispose of the Second Commandment as it is re-interpreted in the light of the gospel. The icons and images that modern Christians are tempted to worship are not pictures painted in oils or watercolours, nor are they statues and statuettes carved in wood or stone. These we may admire and appreciate, or not, as the case may be, but we have no desire to worship them. The idols of our time are those created in the mind, the imagination and the emotions by the impact of the bewildering times in which we live.

The idolatries current in our day are many and various. The God of Afrikaanerdom is constructed out of the God of the Old Testament, scarcely modified by the Father of the Lord Jesus Christ, and concentrating his present purposes on his new Chosen People; and this image has been set in concrete by the experiences of the Great Trek, the persecutions of the British and the opposition of the fierce black tribes who resisted the onward march of God's elect. The God of American electronic evangelism has some resemblance to the God of the New Testament, since he is prepared to forgive sinners in the name of Christ; but he is disfigured by transatlantic bourgeois capitalism into a dealer-out of material success to the born-again and of bankruptcy and disease to the others. The Nazis worshipped, when they worshipped at all, a God compounded of Aryan-Germanic racial consciousness, devotion to German soil, and lust for a world empire.

To come nearer home, in Victorian and Edwardian Britain God was clearly seen to be of British nationality, concerned through his followers (of the same nationality) to control 'the lesser breeds without the law' and give them what he knew to be good for them – exploitation, subservience and more law and order than they could manage for themselves.

Nor can we, the enlightened writer and readers of this book, deny that we also are tempted to make God in our own image, to think of him as the personification of our preconceived ideals and prejudices, creating a parody of God the Father out of our own narrow interests and traditions.

According to Paul, Jesus Christ is 'the icon (the image) of the invisible God (Col. 1.15); and 'we see the glory of God in the face of Jesus Christ' (II Cor. 4.6). These passages could be taken to mean that not only must we condemn pictures and images of God, but must also avoid all speculation and reflection on the nature of God, lest we fall into idolatry, especially since so many idolatries are already in vogue.

But this is an unduly stringent interpretation of Paul. If we are to trust the Book of Acts, he himself made use of Stoic conceptions of God when expounding the gospel to his sophisticated hearers in Athens (Acts 17.27–28). We are surely entitled to develop our idea of God by using the perceptions of Christian thinkers superior to ourselves, and by accepting the insights of those who belong to other schools of thought than our own and to other faiths; and by seeking new ideas from people and peoples not previously consulted on these matters, women, black people and the oppressed nations of Latin America. In these ways our 'scanty thoughts' have been greatly enlarged in recent years, and there is much more to learn. We are saved from idolatry if we see that our ultimate criterion is Christ, the 'icon of the invisible God'. What is consistent with his career, his character and his teaching, or is faithfully and consistently developed from them, is to be, after careful testing, approved, even if it conflicts with individual texts in Old or New Testament, or some traditional ways of thinking. 'In Christ lie hidden all God's treasures of wisdom and knowledge' (Col. 2.3) – and there are vast areas of both still to be brought out and explored.

Thus the positive, Christian meaning of the Second Commandment points to the unfinished theological task of the church. But also to the mental and spiritual discipline of individual Christians by which falsehood and idolatry are excluded, and truth is sought and discovered by openness of mind and constant reference to the mind of Christ.

8 *'You shall not make wrong use of the name of the Lord your God'*

'A rose by any other name would smell as sweet.' This strikes us as a trite and obvious statement. But the ancient Israelites would have violently disagreed if they had heard it. For them the name of a thing or person shows the real character of what or who is named. If by any chance someone has acquired the wrong name, it must be changed or the real name must be added. It was with this in mind that Jesus renamed Simon, the son of Jonas, and he became Simon Peter.

So the name of God shows his nature. It is of supreme importance therefore to know that name. This is why Moses asks urgently, after the vision of the Burning Bush, ' "If I go to the Israelites and tell them that the God of their forefathers has sent me to them, and they ask me his name, what shall I say?" And God answered, "I AM; that is who I am". Tell them that I AM has sent you to them." ' A somewhat mysterious answer, no doubt, later amplified to give God's name as Jahweh, or rather YHWH (we can be fairly sure that the vowels left out by Hebrew custom are a and e – not as our ancestors thought, e and o and a, making 'Jehovah'). Now that the name is given, Moses can pass it on to his people (Ex. 3.13–15). The names 'I AM' and 'Jahweh' emphasize the eternity and present existence of God, and it may be that their very mysteriousness prompted a deeper worship.

To know the name of God gave access not only to his nature but also to his power, and anyone in a 'name-relationship' to him could make use of his power; that is, he could appeal for the use of his power on his behalf. The Third Commandment prohibits the 'wrong use' of the opportunities which God offers his people by disclosing his name.

At its first promulgation, Moses (probably its author) does not seem to have given examples of its wrong use. Perhaps he did not want to encourage specific wrong uses by mentioning them! But later history indicates three ways of misusing the name which were perhaps in his mind and certainly materialized in due course.

The first was the use of the name of God for the purpose of getting one's own way – the attempt to manipulate God. Now it is certain that such an attempt never succeeds, because God cannot be manipulated. But it sometimes seems to succeed. If someone burns an effigy of his enemy, with a prayer to God that his enemy will die, that enemy, if he hears about it, or fears that it has happened, and if he also believes that a curse in the name of God is effective, may then fall ill and die, of extreme fright. If a medicine man or 'wise woman' pronounces a curse, and the curse becomes known, then the cursed man may suffer the same fate. On the other side, if the medicine man or woman makes a potion and prays for the healing of an invalid, and especially if others join in the prayer, the invalid may take fresh heart and recover.

The Third Commandment is a veto on all such practices, that is, on certain forms of what we call 'magic' – black magic when harmful effects are invoked, white magic in the case of good effects. It is difficult, especially in early times, to draw a sharp distinction between magic and religion, and the religion of the Old Testament as described in some passages has magical elements – divination of the future by dreams, for instance – but the attempt to manipulate God, here forbidden (but by no means absent from certain Christian prayers) is a direct contradiction of the religion taught by the Jewish prophets, which had at its heart insistence on the willingness to do and suffer God's will as it was shown to be. One effect of the Third Commandment was the reinforcement of 'prophetic' religion.

The second way of misusing the name of God referred to implicitly by this Commandment is perjury (forbidden again in certain specific areas in the Ninth Commandment) – that is, swearing by the name of God, the most sacred sanction of all, that something has happened which one knows did not happen, or that something is true which one knows not to be true. It is easy to see that civil and social life are virtually impossible if perjury is overlooked when it is discovered.

The third misuse is making vows and not keeping them. Vows in the name of God are frequent in both parts of the Bible – remember Hannah's vow to devote her son, if she had one, to God for his whole life (I Sam. 1.11); remember the vow of forty Jews in Jerusalem not to eat or drink until they had killed Paul (they set an ambush, but did not catch Paul; we are not told whether they starved to death, or could somehow obtain exemption from the vow) (Acts 23.12–14).

A vow was solemnly taken and seriously regarded. To break it was to strike at the roots of the Hebrews' covenant with God.

In the developing history of the Jewish nation, the possibilities of breaking the Third Commandment were seen to be many and various, and questions began to be asked, such as 'Are there any circumstances in which a vow can be broken, for instance when it is not physically possible to keep it?' Was the young David guilty when he remained in the camp of the Philistines, that is, continued in rebellion against King Saul, after he had sworn never to injure the king, the Lord's anointed, and the Lord's anointed did not receive him back into favour (see I Sam. 26, 27)? In the end, after the Exile, it seemed prudent not to utter the name of the Lord at all, in case one should unwittingly misuse it, and from then on Jahweh has never been named in Jewish worship; when the word occurs in the text of the Old Testament, the rabbi uses a title of God which is not his real name. The practice began in prudence and caution; it is continued today in reverence, lest God's holy name be trivialized or profaned.

The Third Commandment has now passed from its original status as a regulation for the life of the Jewish nation into the conscience of humankind, influenced as it is by Jewish and Christian traditions.

We do not ascribe the same significance or power to the name of God as did the ancient Hebrews; we have disclaimed all belief in magic and we make fewer vows in general. But we retain vows for those who enter a monastic order or the estate of marriage, and we demand an oath of allegiance from members of the Armed Forces, certain officers in church and state, and we exact an oath 'to speak the truth, the whole truth and nothing but the truth' from those who give evidence in a court of law (though here certain exemptions are allowed).

Perjury is a criminal offence, and is morally frowned on by the majority of people. Monastic vows are treated very seriously still, though men and women *can* be released from them. But recent matrimonial legislation, which contemplates the breaking of marriage vows with equanimity, clearly tends in the direction of devaluing these vows, and perhaps makes it necessary to substitute another word for the vows made in a marriage service, since the undertaking now given by many people is now different.

Thus the Third Commandment may be said to deal with a reduced number of likely misuses of the divine name. But in post-biblical times, and up to the present in those circles where the reality of God is still affirmed, it has come to cover something which Moses and his successors probably did not have in mind – swearing in the sense of the use of swearwords in conversation and speech-making (and therefore in drama of all kinds).

In the twenties of this century Robert Graves wrote a book called *Lars Porsena, or the Future of Swearing*. (Lars Porsena, it will be remembered, according to Macaulay's *Lays of Ancient Rome*, swore by the Nine Gods, whoever *they* were.) In this he shows that swearwords originate with God, sex or the lavatory. So far as the present author's limited knowledge of these matters goes, this is still true.

Against the argument, widely endorsed, that swearwords are often more expressive and forceful than ordinary words, and have the additional element of surprise when they come from the lips of someone who does not usually use them, the objections to these modern sorts of swearing are: 1. they show an inability or unwillingness to control feelings which are best kept in check for the purpose of personal relationships; 2. they show a serious poverty of vocabulary, especially when repeated every minute or so; 3. they lack precise meaning and obtain their force by plain, crude exaggeration (the word 'damn' is a case in point; it means 'consign to hell'); 4. they sometimes call up pictures of behaviour which are not suitable for public evocation even in words.

But do they infringe the Third Commandment? Words connected with sex and the lavatory cannot really be said to do so. To lace one's conversation with 'God' and 'Christ' (and 'bloody', which has a theological origin) frequently repeated, is a quite meaningless thing to do for those who do not believe in God or Christ or the Virgin Mary, though the words themselves retain a surprising amount of force in a secular age. But is it a misuse of the name of God? The answer must be Yes, since it trivializes what is a matter of supreme importance whether one believes in God and Christ or not. The question of God's existence must always remain the most important in human experience; to refer to it casually or indifferently or contemptuously is to show that one is culpably, or perhaps ignorantly, unaware of that fact. But is God insulted or dishonoured? Is Christ insulted or dishonoured? Surely not. They are subject to far more serious 'insults' and 'dishonourings'; they show no sign of hurt or displeasure, and their love for humankind is not affected or diminished. To misuse the name of God may well insult or hurt men and women and children, because their cherished beliefs are attacked; and this is a thing that responsible people try to avoid doing. But God himself, and Christ himself, do not need to be protected from insult, calumny or blasphemy. There is on other grounds a strong case for the abolition of the laws of blasphemy. But if they are retained, it is not for the sake of God or religion, but of human people.

Jesus' reinterpretation of the Third Commandment for those who enter the Kingdom of God seems at first sight to amount to a negation of it, but it does not really do so.

'You have learned that our forefathers were told, "Do not break your oath," and "Oaths sworn to the Lord must be kept." But what

I say to you is this: You are not to swear at all – plain "Yes" or "No"
is all you need to say; anything beyond that comes from the devil'
(Matt. 5.33–37).

In the Kingdom of God there is no need to take oaths by the name
of God. We speak the truth and give our evidence without invoking
any sanctions in case we do not; we make our promises simply and
plainly, and we keep them; we are loyal to our country and our
church without requiring either God or our fellow human beings to
hear us declare our loyalty; we are faithful to our wives or husbands
without calling heaven and earth to witness our vows.

Thus in the Kingdom of God those who know us trust us, believe
in us, and rely on our word once given.

This is, plainly, the ideal state of affairs, and it really exists within
a genuinely Christian community; indeed, it is a criterion of such a
community. But as we appraise the Christian meaning of the Third
Commandment for the actual world in which we live, two considerations need to be borne in mind. The first is that even those who
live in the Kingdom of God sometimes lapse into a condition –
temporary, we hope – which puts them outside the Kingdom of
God. They may become unreliable in keeping their promises, or
their relations with their spouses. They may think that the way to
guard themselves against such lapses is to take a solemn oath or make
a solemn vow that they will never be unfaithful. In view of the
frailty of human nature the church has traditionally instructed its
members to take this course, even though it is less than the ideal.

The other consideration is that those who live in the Kingdom of
God live also in 'the kingdom of this world'; and in the latter kingdom – that is, in every known human society – no one, however
honest he or she may know himself or herself to be, is trusted to tell
the truth unless he or she is bound by a solemn oath (and often by
penalties attached to a breach of that oath).

Members of the Society of Friends are reluctant to swear an oath
in any circumstances, and the law in many countries frees them
from doing so on the ground of their conscientious belief. But most
Christians are willing to compromise, and take the oath of allegiance
to the Crown when so required, and swear by Almighty God when

they stand in the witness box.

But the word 'compromise' raises many Christian hackles. Compromise, surely, is alien to the whole spirit of the Christian gospel? No, it cannot be. There are bad compromises and good compromises, and the word needs to be saved from its ill odour. It is a bad compromise when we suppress the truth or change our opinion or our attitude merely to please someone else or to keep our reputation, or our purse, or our position in society, intact. As a general rule it is a good compromise when two opposite courses of action are put before us for us to choose between them, each of them likely to cause some good and some evil; and we choose the one that in our opinion is likely to cause the more good and the less evil.

This is the kind of choice with which we are regularly faced as we live in two kingdoms, and under two sets of laws. In the present case, if we refuse to swear an oath of allegiance when required by law, the post in which we wish to serve will not be ours and our witness to the truth will not be accepted. If we swear, we shall disobey the command to refrain from every kind of oath. How do we choose? Surely we should choose the course of action which will do more to promote the purposes of the Kingdom of God, even though we may be aware that some harm will be done by it.

This is a conclusion which may be distasteful to many Christians, since they aim at obeying the teaching of Christ without any kind of compromise or reservation. But as we go through those Commandments which deal with the relations of persons with persons, and of persons with society, we shall find many points at which the 'principle of good compromise' will be invoked, and can be tested. In the sphere of personal relations it has to be applied with great sensitivity towards the feelings and welfare of all the people involved.

9 'Remember to keep the Sabbath Day holy'

If, as seems likely, the Fourth Commandment was not part of the original package of Mosaic legislation, the most probable cause of its later insertion was the influence of Babylonian religion. During the Babylonian epoch, from 605 to 538 BC, the Hebrews perforce had frequent contact with the imperial power, usually of a humiliating kind. Their most disastrous encounter was in 586 BC, when King Nebuchadrezzar captured Jerusalem, razed city and temple to the ground, and deported the majority of the population to live as third-class citizens in the country round Babylon. During their painful exile, the Hebrews were determined for the most part to maintain their own identity and religion, but they could not escape the impact of Babylonian customs, and it was in these circumstances, probably, that they adopted the custom of a festival every seven days, and of calling it a 'Sabbath'. The word may have come from the Babylonian *sapattu*, which was a monthly festival, held on the day of the full moon; weekly festivals were also kept in Babylon, though not with so much pomp as the *sapattu*.

If this was the origin of the Jewish Sabbath – and we cannot be quite certain – it did not determine the way in which the Hebrews celebrated the weekly festival when they returned to their own country, liberated by Cyrus, the Persian king who had put an end to the Babylonian Empire. They proceeded to associate it with the day of rest which Jahweh enjoyed after the strenuous six days of creation, and to add a humanitarian flavour by prescribing a respite from work for man, woman and beast. Thus established, the Sabbath steadily became the hallmark of Jewish religion and statehood in distinction from all the peoples living around, so much so that in the Maccabaean wars of the second century BC, many Jews were willing to be killed rather than break the Sabbath by fighting (a fact of which their enemies took full advantage on at least one occasion).

But the veto on work was not so easy to interpret as it seemed at first. Certain things, it soon appeared, had to be done on the Sabbath, and they could not be denied the title of work – looking after animals and serving meals in particular (though much of the cooking could no doubt be done in advance). So the rabbis were called upon to decide what was forbidden and what was not, and over the years they drew up a formidable list of prohibitions, permissions, dispensations and exemptions. By the time of Jesus the list was so complex and so difficult to memorize that many of the ordinary people did not bother themselves very much about keeping every item of the Sabbath laws, and were contemptuously called 'sinners' by the Pharisees as a consequence.

Jesus himself was taken to task by the Pharisees for healing a lame man on the Sabbath, and for allowing his disciples, on another Sabbath, to pluck the ears of corn on the edge of a cornfield, rub them in their hands and eat them (this was perfectly allowable on the other days of the week). His response was to show how absurd it was to refrain from doing good on the Sabbath; and he went on to declare that the Sabbath was made for the benefit of the human race, not the human race for the benefit of the Sabbath. No doubt he and his disciples continued to do what they had been doing. It may well be that the more liberal-minded of the Pharisees agreed with them (not all the Pharisees, by any means, were narrow-minded and repressive).

After the death and resurrection of Jesus the Christian church, at first made up mostly of Jews, continued many Jewish customs, including the Sabbath, but they also added their own, notably that of 'breaking bread' together, though not yet on a specific day of the week. But as the church gradually became more and more Gentile in composition, the Jewish customs (such as circumcision) for the most part were dropped, and Christian customs took pride of place. Most visibly of all the seventh day of the week, the Sabbath, was replaced by the first day of the week, the day of the Resurrection, the day of the coming of the Holy Spirit, Sunday. The change was taking place in New Testament times: Paul broke bread with the Christians in Troas on the first day of the week (Acts 20.7). Soon it was universal, except that some Jewish Christians kept the Sabbath as well for a time.

There is no good evidence that the early Christians refrained from working on the first day of the week. How could they, without losing their livelihood? They probably celebrated the Lord's Supper early in the morning of Sunday, and then went off to their daily occupation; or, perhaps more often in the earlier period, they ate a common meal after the day's work was over and went on to celebrate the Lord's Supper. But when the church was legalized by the Roman Empire and its activities officially encouraged, the proper way to spend Sunday was soon prescribed by imperial edict in the interests of the church. In an edict of 321 AD the Emperor Constantine ordered abstention from work on Sundays for townspeople, but allowed work on the farm. From then on the Sunday laws became gradually stricter, with penalties attached, until they were so strict that it became necessary to give many dispensations to people who simply had to work. The priestly and homiletic activities of the clergy were not, of course, regarded as work (nor are they now!).

By the time of the Reformation attendance at Mass had long been compulsory; the rest of the day could be used in strictly defined ways. But it is very evident that the weakness, or strength, of human nature proved capable of stretching the laws in various directions, and the spirit of the laws was often infringed.

The Reformers determined to check the widespread abuses by laying down strict rules for their own congregations, and nowhere more repressively than in England and Scotland (where, perhaps, the people were more dissolute than elsewhere). In Geneva John Calvin allowed certain games on Sunday, and occasionally played bowls himself. In Scotland, under John Knox, such concessions were unthinkable.

In 1595 a certain Nicholas Bound, an English Puritan, brought out *The True Doctrine of the Sabbath*, and in this book and in subsequent Puritan writing Sunday is explicitly identified with the Jewish Sabbath, as it had been virtually identified with it before. King James I took a moderate line on the matter in his *Book of Sports* (1618), allowing archery and dancing, and disallowing more brutish sports. But the Puritans, once in power, had no use for moderation or for King James, and Sunday was assimilated to the Sabbath by law. The Restoration and the eighteenth century went in the direction of greater liberty, but the Lord's Day Observance Act of 1781 reversed this trend. Nineteenth-century Christianity, under Evangelical and Tractarian influence, insisted on the restriction of Sunday to worship, acts of charity and piety and the reading of certain carefully selected books; the resultant tedium for many sections of the population was not regarded as important by the authorities in church or state. So violent reaction was bound to come in due course. At the same time social legislation restricted the allowable hours of Sunday work; such legislation was the good side of the sabbatarian coin.

The situation has now changed irreversibly, except in remote parts of Scotland, under the impact of industrial and technological revolution, the development of sophisticated entertainment, the popularity of professional and amateur sport, and the all-pervasiveness of secularism. It is just no longer possible to enforce the old laws of Sunday observance, except in certain spheres, and the attempts to do so have led only to confusion in law and practice; there is little reason to doubt that in due course all restrictive Sunday legislation will be swept away, in spite of the efforts of many church-people and others to 'keep Sunday special'.

Until fairly recently, perhaps until the end of the Second World War, the command to keep Sunday 'holy' was accepted as part of the law of God, and the numerous people in every rank of society who broke it were quick to make excuses, and acted with an inward sense of guilt and an outward show of bravado. Now no longer. People 'break the Sabbath' with a clear conscience.

Something valuable, however, remains from the collapse of the institution. It is still ingrained in the modern conscience that we ought to keep one day in the week free from work – for family life, or recreational activities, or just for rest – and allow and encourage other people to do the same. Most people in the United Kingdom probably agree that this is the only part of the Fourth Commandment that remains valid, and they would support this part for medical, psychological and economic, rather than religious reasons.

The question now arises: how are those whose supreme allegiance is the Kingdom of God to observe Sunday in the confusing and confused conditions of our time? Before we can attempt to give an answer to that, a very important matter, long obscured in the history of the church, and of English churches in particular, needs to be cleared up.

It is sadly the case that many early Christian teachers showed a very strong tendency to turn the gospel which Jesus preached, and for which he died – a gospel of the free grace of God offering forgiveness to sinners – into a New Law, which like the old Law had to be obeyed in detail if salvation was to be gained. This tendency is already to be observed in the Gospel of Matthew; it becomes stronger and stronger in the second and third centuries, and has in many ways continued through history, needing Augustine of Hippo, Martin Luther, John Wesley and others to protest against it in the name of the gospel as Jesus and Paul preached it, and to lead the church back on to the right path.

Sunday, as we have seen, gradually took the place of the Sabbath in the Christian communities. It was a new festival, to celebrate the Resurrection and the new life of Christ, a day for thanksgiving and a joyful eucharist. Naturally it took over some of the features of the Jewish Sabbath, and the imperial edict forbidding work was very welcome to those Christians who had campaigned for it. But the 'legalistic tendency' took hold of it, and, although its original purpose was still affirmed, and, at least formally, carried out, that purpose was gradually overlaid by a growing number of prohibitions, until

Sunday deserved the comment which Jesus made about the Sabbath, that it was made for the human race and not the other way round. Legalism, expelled through the front door, had slipped in at the back.

There were bound to be popular reactions against this, in the form of buffoonery and licentiousness; so an even stricter régime than before was imposed – later-mediaeval excesses followed by the zeal of the Reformers. Then came another reaction in the shape of obscene stage plays on Sundays under the Stuarts, and these were followed by the excessive rigours of the Puritans. Then another reaction and counter-reaction; extravagance and ribaldry under the Restoration, scarcely controlled during the eighteenth century, followed by the renewed Puritanism of the Evangelical Revival. This last extreme helped to create the Victorian Sunday, which has been steadily whittled away – not violently destroyed – until only a few traces of it remain.

This is a sad story of constant oscillation. Looking back on it, we can surely see that many of its absurdities and much of its bitterness – indeed, perhaps the historical see-saw itself – could have been avoided if the prime mistake had not been made of virtually identifying the Christian Sunday with the Jewish Sabbath: Sunday was meant to replace the Sabbath, while taking on board its best elements, not to imitate it and perpetuate it.

If all this is borne in mind, it becomes a little easier to discuss what Christians should do, and not do, on Sunday! It is even worthwhile to try to look at the question with entirely fresh eyes, although we cannot easily eliminate the gut feelings (and prejudices?) that we have inherited.

It goes without saying (since it has been constantly said by the New Testament and the unanimous tradition of the church) that worship in the community of the Kingdom, the church, must have pride of place – a full diet of worship, with sacrament, prayer, preaching and praising. This is why all churches are rightly concerned at present about the quality of their worship, and seeking to eliminate anything slipshod, mechanical, sensationalistic or merely dull.

Next in place comes Christian teaching, both in worship and apart from it. Whether Religious Education in schools is good or bad (and there is much variation), the church has its duty to nurture in mind and body children preceeding from baptism to the fullness of membership in confirmation. It also has the duty of adult Christian education. This has long been neglected, as is shown by the profound ignorance of Christian doctrine acknowledged by many people who have been faithful churchgoers all their lives. It is unrealistic to suppose that this is best done on weekdays; only a few people, in the nature of the case, can take advantage of the excellent weekday facilities offered by many churches and para-church organizations and universities. Sunday, in church, is the only time and place not cluttered up innumerable calls on crowded timetables. Perhaps the American churches, which invite people of all ages on Sunday morning to suitable 'Sunday Schools', have got this right.

Otherwise, a Christian is surely free to take his or her 'rest and relaxation' in the form of creative activity, the enjoyment of family life, or just in sleep – so long as he or she does not by so doing force people to work who do not wish to work, and so long as he or she takes part, if possible, in the 'work' which his or her activity involves. And if there are some activities which seem 'wrong' on Sundays, is it possible that they are wrong on weekdays also?

But we live in a society which for the most part has no use for, no interest in, and no understanding of, the priorities of Christians. Have Christians the right to support the enactment or maintenance of laws which impose on society various prohibitions which are meaningless to most of their fellow citizens? Surely not. But they do have the right to argue that Sunday laws should not interfere with the freedom of those who wish to spend Sunday in a Christian way, or exploit those who will have to work longer hours as the laws are relaxed, or infringe the conscientious conviction of many people (and certainly not of Christians only) that everyone needs, and is entitled to, a day which is different from the rest of the week. Perhaps someone, some time, will come up with a bill for Parliament which satisfies these conditions!

The first four Commandments concentrate on our duties to God, the last six on our duties to one another.

The Fifth Commandment, to love one's parents, with its corollaries for the maintenance of a close-knit family life, has been one of the solid foundations of Judaism from the time of Moses until now. Through its chequered history, and not least in the periods of bitter persecution, the cohesiveness of the family has helped to keep the nation together as no other nation has been kept together in the annals of human life. This cohesiveness has been shown – and is still shown – in the homes of Jews, not only when they have lived in their own land; but also in the long periods of 'diaspora', when families have been divided and scattered, but have nevertheless preserved their inward unity. All this is largely due to the observance of the Fifth Commandment.

The Jewish family in the Old Testament was patriarchal, and so it continued to be in post-Biblical times (how far this is still the case it is not for non-Jews to decide, though it is clear that nowadays by long-standing custom a widowed 'matriarch' is a very powerful person). The father was the undisputed head of the family (or of the 'household', when the slaves and hired workers are included, as they often are); under him was the mother; under her were the children; and this structure remained fixed until the father died, and the headship passed to his eldest son. This means that the honour due, according to the Fifth Commandment, to father and mother was not equal. To honour the father implied obedience, as well as affection, and care in old age. To honour the mother implied obedience to the mother as she expressed the father's wishes, and not to her in her own right; and also affection and care in old age.

There are certainly some exceptional women in the Old Testament who take the lead in emergencies of the nation – Miriam, for instance, Deborah and Esther. But the Old Testament draws attention to them precisely because they were exceptional, and they do not damage the general patriarchal pattern (even anti-feminists today, of necessity, allow for the occasional appearance of exceptional women). According to the law as it developed, the wife was the property of the husband, who could divorce her at will; and it was never laid down that he should restrict himself to one wife, although monogamy seems to have gradually prevailed, and to have become universal by the time of Jesus.

So strong and exemplary has been the influence of Jewish family life that it has played a great part in the formation of Western civilization. Greece and Rome, the other two cultures out of which our own culture has grown, contributed relatively little to the idea and practice of the family. And now that the Western family pattern is in the course of radical change, it may well be that the Jewish family will survive the demise of the institution which it helped to bring into existence.

But for the present, at least, the Fifth Commandment and its implications remain part of the moral consciousness of Western society. In spite of the frequency of divorce, the vast increase in the number of one-parent families, and of children who distance themselves, psychologically as well as geographically, from their parents, most of our contemporaries inwardly acknowledge their family obligations, and when they do not fulfil them, without having an excuse with which they can satisfy themselves, they are haunted by a sense of guilt for the rest of their lives. This may seem an exaggerated statement, but much modern literature bears witness to its truth; the guilt-ridden son or daughter tortured by conflicting desires is a familiar character in fiction.

In one important respect the modern Western conscience – including in this case, that of the Jews – has drawn a very proper inference from the Fifth Commandment. Until fairly recently, the care of parents as they grew old was entirely the responsibility of their children, with no help from outside except from charitable institutions (if any were available to help). The complex conditions of twentieth-century life have made this increasingly difficult, and in recent years virtually impossible in many cases; this has been brought about by smaller houses, daughters and daughters-in-law with careers of their own and domiciles far from the parental home, and, not insignificantly, the tendency of the old to live longer. So modern governments, out of a sense of obligation (as we may hope – not many votes are yet at stake, though the number grows), have first of all provided pensions, and later, assistance in providing accommodation, for the elderly, together with various small financial concessions. As the number of pensioners increases, state assistance has failed to keep up with the need, but the national conscience has been aroused. This social and moral development often places the younger generation in a dilemma; should the old people be kept in their family, or 'sent to a home'? In either case they wonder whether they have obeyed the Commandment to 'honour your father and mother'. Old and young suffer much from this.

So much for this Commandment as a continuing part of the moral law. How is it transformed in the Kingdom of God?

The answer is not so simple as we should like. We have the surprising, not often noticed fact that Jesus does not seem to lay much stress on the honouring of parents or on family life in general. During his visit to Jerusalem at the age of twelve (Luke 2.41–52) he caused great anxiety to his parents, but was not himself worried, it seems; when his mother and brothers asked him to come and see them while he was teaching (Mark 3.31–35) he did not readily do so; and we have his declaration that anyone who puts his parents above the demands of the Kingdom cannot be his disciple (Luke 14.26 – which actually states that we must hate our parents!). In all these instances a downgrading of the obligations to parents seems to be implied. We must not explain away these passages by saying (as preachers sometimes do) that Jesus did not really mean what he said,

but was being ironical; but we *can* say that he took for granted the
basic Jewish tradition of honouring one's parents (as he does
explicitly in Mark 7.10), and then pointed out, in striking, even
exaggerated terms that there is something even higher in authority
than family life, the Kingdom of God, which calls for a total
allegiance.

Within the family, thus seen to be under the authority of the
Kingdom, Jesus affirms the parity of men and women, and so of
fathers and mothers. This is not immediately obvious, for it was not
fully grasped by his followers, and therefore is not brought out in
the New Testament epistles. Paul does indeed say in Gal. 3.28 that
in Christ there is no such thing as male and female, 'for you are one
person in Christ'. From this it surely follows that neither sex is
superior to the other, any more than Jews and Greeks, in Christ, are
superior to each other; it follows from this that fathers and mothers
are to be given parity of honour. But for the most part he falls back
into the Old Testament notion of male headship, which he several
times emphasizes (e.g. I Cor. 11.3); and the First Epistle of Peter
expresses the same view (I Peter 3.1).

But the rise of women to important offices very early in the life
of the church (e.g. Phoebe in Corinth, Rom. 16.1) shows that a different current of thought was blowing strongly. If we look back to
the Gospels we can see that this current goes back to the practice and
teaching of Jesus himself. Not only did he treat women in exactly
the same way as he treated men (a characteristic of his which deeply
shocked many of his contemporaries), he rejected out of hand, for
those who had entered the Kingdom of God, all notions of superior-
ity and headship, and therefore by direct implication the headship of
man over woman: 'in this world, kings lord it over their subjects;
and those in authority are called their country's "Benefactors". Not
so among you: on the contrary, the highest among you must bear
himself like the youngest, the chief of you like a servant' (Luke
22.27). Nothing could be plainer than this; and it is hard to see how
the churches, with this text and the example of Jesus in front of
them, have reconciled the maintenance of hierarchies of power and
the continued subordination of women with their Christian think-

ing. Jesus surely has ruled out patriarchy (and, for that matter, matriarchy as well) in the Kingdom of God. It is worthy of note that Luke, who understood this better than Paul, places the Magnificat, with its denunciation of power structures, on the lips of a woman – and a woman who speaks to Christians with great authority.

It is in the family where this Christian truth is at its most important, and where, alas, it is most rarely put into practice. But when equal honour, or, as we should say, respect, is given by children to each parent, their mother and father will show equal respect to one another. For these things to happen, or to continue when the children are growing up, the parents need to earn the children's respect. For the relation of respect between parents and children is meant to be reciprocal, avoiding domination and possessiveness, since Jesus in contrast with the customs of his time welcomed children and asserted that they were members of the Kingdom of God (Mark 10.14). So the Christian family (*not* the Victorian family) is a community of persons, in which each member treats every other as a person in his or her own right, helping and encouraging him or her to be truly himself or herself, developing and exercising the gifts given to each. Enhanced and deepened by the maturing of sexual love and by natural affection and loyalty, it is a unique (yes, the right word is 'unique') opportunity for the flowering and practice of neighbour-love – and the best prophylactic against the spreading disease of social disintegration.

11 'You shall not commit murder'

The Sixth Commandment does not concern itself with killing one's enemies in war (as we have seen in an earlier chapter), or with any killing ordered by the state; nor is it a veto on killing animals. It simply and plainly forbids personal, private killing – killing for personal gain, or as an act of vengeance, or as an expression of sexual or other jealousy, or of ambition, or of sheer hatred, or as a result of going berserk, whether it be premeditated or on a sudden impulse. It is the prohibition of the taking of human life by those not authorized to do so.

As such it commands the agreement of all human societies, and does not require the sanctions of the Decalogue, since all human societies enforce it in their own different ways. It remains unchallenged in the conscience of the human race. The one exception ever made is killing in self-defence, and this only within strict limits.

But in recent times even this straightforward prohibition has become complicated. Abortion, until recently regarded as a criminal offence and as contrary to the moral law, is now legalized in several countries, under certain conditions and restrictions. Is it indeed contrary to the moral law nevertheless? Is it a breach of the Sixth Commandment?

The theological argument which has raged around this issue has usually centred on the question: at what point does a human embryo acquire a soul? At conception, or during the course of pregnancy, or at birth? This particular question has troubled Christian authorities from time to time through many centuries, but the weight of evidence now points to the conclusion that the Bible does not teach that we *have* souls at all, but rather that we *are* souls, i.e. that 'soul' is one ancient term for what we call personality (another being, rather confusingly, 'body'). When God in the Book of Ezekiel (18.4 AV) says 'all souls are mine', he means 'all *persons* are mine', in our language.

But the question remains. Is abortion the killing of a human person? When do we begin to be human persons? If the beginning of our life as human beings is at our conception, then to destroy a foetus is murder – and is presumably not justified in any circumstances, while a miscarriage is not just a misfortune for the mother but the death of a person. If, on the other hand, we do not begin to be persons until we are born as beings separate from our mothers, then abortion is in principle justified, if there are good reasons, such as the mental or physical health of the mother, or the prospect of severe and permanent mental or physical derangement of the child that would otherwise be born. This is the way in which the issue should be stated.

It is too soon to make a definitive judgment on an issue that still divides responsible people, Christian and non-Christian.

Another complicating factor is the issue of euthanasia. This also has been universally condemned until recently, and is still illegal everywhere, though sometimes surreptitiously practised with impunity. The question here is: when does human life cease? Always and only at death, or may it not cease when incurable illness has stopped the exercise of all human faculties while the heart continues to beat? In the latter case, there is a strong argument for euthanasia, if some way can be found of ensuring that it is the deliberate or previously expressed wish of the patient and that the process of dying is demonstrably irreversible.

But this question, too, is still debated among responsible and well-informed people.

There is one piece of modern legislation, reflecting a sharpened social conscience, in which the application of the Sixth Commandment approaches the standard set by the teaching of Jesus, and that is the law passed in several Western countries (not in all) abolishing capital punishment. The reasons for its passing are partly practical: the discovery that the fear of execution does not diminish the number of murders committed, and the uneasy knowledge that miscarriages of justice and executions of innocent people may occur, and have occurred, even under the best available legal systems. But there is a moral ingredient also: the perception that the principle of an eye for an eye, however subtle its presentation, is the relic of a half-Christian, half-barbarian society. There are still strident voices calling for the return of hanging; it will be a sign of moral deterioration if they have their way.

As might be expected, we move into a different world of thought when we look at the Sixth Commandment in the light of the Kingdom of God. Jesus challenges received morality and the Decalogue in two important respects (they are well-known and have been referred to already).

The first challenge is made when he puts 'nursing anger against my brother' on the same level as murder (Matt. 5.21–22). The New English Bible is probably right in translating the Greek word by 'nursing anger', not, as the older versions do, by 'being angry'. Jesus is not saying that a sudden and/or temporary anger with someone is equivalent to murdering him or her. He is thinking of a bitter grievance, or desire for vengeance, or deep hatred, long cherished but never actually given outward expression (except perhaps in words, 'I'll kill him if I get the chance'), probably through fear of the consequences.

In the Kingdom, then, the cherished inner desire is as bad as its fulfilment – a teaching which demands, it may well seem, more from us than we are able to give. In 'the kingdom of this world' the desire for revenge is regarded as wholly allowable, even commendable; the willingness to forgive, as in the case of some of those bereaved by the Enniskillen bombing in 1987, is thought to be no doubt admirable, but unintelligible. Even members of the Kingdom of God must agree that such forgiveness does not come naturally, but only after a long and deep awareness of the forgiving love of God.

The other challenge is yet more searching; the command to love one's enemies and pray for one's persecutors (Matt. 5.43–44). This, be it noted, requires not only the conquest of anger against certain people, but positive love for them – the same love as we are called upon to have for all our other neighbours. Once again the impossible is required of us, and then made possible by the contemplation of the undiscriminating love of God for all his creatures.

Some Christians hold that the command to love one's enemies has a purely private and personal reference. They would say that it is only those who cherish enmity towards us within our own circle, or within the community to which we belong, or even our nation, whom we are called upon to love. If our nation is attacked by a foreign enemy and defends itself, they say, the command of Jesus does not apply.

Others find this an intolerable and impracticable limitation. If we are to follow the example of God's universal love, then the enemies to be loved must include all those who act in a hostile way towards us, our country's enemies as well as our own.

If we take the second view we have a clear and painful case of the interaction between the kingdom of this world and the Kingdom of God. Our country may command us to kill, or help to kill, its enemies, and even pronounce that it is treachery for us to refuse to do so (not all countries allow for the possibility of 'conscientious objection'). But on the other hand we have the clear command of Jesus.

This is a dilemma from which no one can escape. The absolute pacifist may claim to do so, but in fact it cannot be done. For if I refuse to join the armed forces in time of war, I am weakening the forces arrayed against the enemy, if only very slightly, and thus abetting the killing of my own countrypeople. I can even be said in that case to love my enemies more than my friends! If I seek to diminish this reproach by tending the wounded or helping in the growth and distribution of food, I am helping my country to defeat and kill the enemy.

But if I 'join up' I am committed to the killing of as many of the enemy as possible, in clear breach of the command to love them.

I may seek to diminish this reproach by fighting always with the purpose of re-establishing peace as soon as possible. I may hold that to allow the enemy to triumph would result in the killing of more people than will lose their lives in war, and in the continuation of injustice, cruelty and oppression into the indefinite future, but I cannot eliminate the reproach altogether.

In other words, the Christian, however genuine he or she is in the desire to obey the Lord, is bound to compromise one way or another by choosing the lesser of two evils, believing it to be also the greater of two goods. Whichever course of action is chosen, the 'principle of good compromise' has been brought into play.

This dilemma has not yet been satisfactorily resolved, and Christians who interpret the 'laws of the Kingdom' in different ways must respect one another. Paradoxically, the situation is eased when the war in prospect is a nuclear one. For such a war would entirely destroy both, or all contestants, and the participation in it could scarcely be called the lesser of two evils, still less the greater of two goods.

It is important that Christians should not be so preoccupied with the issue of pacifism and non-pacifism that they forget the purpose of the command to love one's enemies. This surely is that one's enemies should become one's friends, and share in the building of a human society in which war is no longer seen as a legitimate way to promote national interests.

12 'You shall not commit adultery'

The original intention of the Seventh Commandment, which no doubt goes back to the Mosaic edition of the Decalogue, was to restrain any and every man from taking the property of another man, in this case his wife. It was more about property than sex. But as time went on, although the idea of a wife as property was never quite lost in Old Testament times, other more exalted (as we should say) considerations came in. The Book of Genesis furthered the idea of a wife as a 'partner' to her husband (Gen. 2.18) (not as 'helpmeet', as the older versions suggest, implying an inferior position); and adultery was even sometimes seen as the breaking up of a personal relationship. The prophet Hosea, who had the misfortune to marry someone who turned out to be an adulteress, agonized about receiving back the unfaithful woman whom he dearly loved, and eventually did so (Hos. 3.1–5) – and the notion of regaining a property was certainly not in the forefront of his mind.

The Old Testament prescribed death by stoning for adulterers and adulteresses (Deut. 22.22), and although in later times this sentence was rarely carried out (an eye-witness was needed, and this was no doubt difficult), the offence itself continued to be thought of as one of major criminality.

Yet we must be careful not to read back into the Old Testament the denigration of sex in itself which became current in the history of the Christian church. There is nothing in the Law or the Prophets to suggest that it is anything but a gift of God, which like other gifts of God can be used well or badly. The presence of the Song of Songs in the canon is a clear proof that the Hebrew religion accepted sex in this way. Certain sexual activities were prohibited and punished, of course, but sex itself was not; sexuality in fact is presupposed to be an integral part of human personality. In Christian times it has been largely thought that adultery, in the sense of sexual intercourse between a married person and someone of the other sex, married or single, is plainly wrong, that it is forbidden not only in the Decalogue but in all systems of morality, and that there is nothing more to be said.

This is apparently the view of nearly all moralists, theologians and biblical commentators, who pass over the matter in very few words. But there is, in fact, much more to the matter than they recognize. The urge to adultery can reach the deepest springs of human sexuality, and raise the profoundest of ethical questions. It has always been fiercely defended by those involved; the psychologists, the dramatists and the novelists know better than the theologians and the moralists that it cannot be summarily disposed of by legislation or moral censure, and they have now created an atmosphere in which the veto on adultery has only a precarious place in the modern conscience.

It is usual to regard the teaching of Jesus on marriage, adultery and divorce as something quite separate from the rest of his teaching. This is a mistake. Like everything else that he taught, his sayings on this subject must be taken in the context of the Kingdom of God; and, in particular, of the injunction to love our neighbour as ourselves. The relations between men and women, and between husband and wife, since they affect the whole of human experience at so profound a level, form an area in which neighbour-love is most especially called for. If it is not shown there, its apparent presence elsewhere may be bogus.

In the Kingdom of God, according to Jesus, a lustful eye cast on a woman by a man is equivalent to adultery (Matt. 5.28). Presumably a lustful eye cast on a man by a woman comes under the same condemnation. This is a teaching which if taken literally and seriously would increase the number of adulterers and adulteresses to an alarming and incalculable extent. But it has never in fact been so taken (we tend to take literally those sayings which fit in with our preconceived ideas, and not those which do not!). Perhaps we are right in saying (rather conveniently, it must be acknowledged) that this is one of the cases where Jesus deliberately exaggerates, in order to make his point about uncontrolled desire, or desire controlled only by the difficulty of satisfying it. But it would be more honest to regard it as one of the extreme demands of the Kingdom.

And it is a demand which springs from the command to love our neighbours as ourselves. Not only adultery, but the desire to commit it breaks that command. For in the Kingdom the age-old prohibition of adultery takes a new form. Adultery (and the desire for it) is no longer a form of robbery (for the wife, as Jesus thought about women, is certainly not a piece of property). It is no longer just a breach of contract or loyalty, nor just the breaking up of a partnership. It is a plain denial of neighbour-love. The offence is not purely physical, it is personal. The integrity, the wholeness of a personal relationship, is shattered by it.

It is not really possible to tell whether Jesus allowed divorce on the grounds of adultery or not. In Matt. 5.21–22 he does; in Mark 10.9–12 he forbids divorce altogether – within the Kingdom of God (he is not speaking of human society in general).

But this leads on to the consideration of many other matters not unrelated to adultery, and to the addition of a third section to this chapter. The church in its history has tended to observe the outward form of Jesus' teaching on marriage, adultery and divorce, and to neglect its inward meaning. We have to ask how this degeneration occurred. Paul did not have a very high opinion of marriage, and preferred celibacy. But this is understandable in view of his conviction that the coming of the Lord and the end of all things were imminent. But he did show signs of understanding the relationship of equality between husband and wife (I Cor. 7.3–4), as well as maintaining the 'headship' of the husband; and if he, or a disciple of his, was the author of the Letter to the Ephesians, he at least began to interpret the marital relationship in terms of loving others as ourselves (Eph. 5.25–29).

He has often been charged with regarding sex as evil in itself. But this is a misunderstanding of his use of the word 'flesh'. He certainly regarded 'the flesh' as evil, but he meant by the word the drive within us to have our own way in personal, social, financial and political matters; not carnal desire.

After the time of Paul, when his direct influence and that of the other apostles were withdrawn, the church attracted to itself certain ways of thinking, mostly from further East, which were alien to the teaching of Christ and of Paul. These 'gnostic' views, as they are called, denied all value to material things, and to sex and the body in particular. They found a welcome in many Christian circles, which were appalled by the loose morals of society around them, and felt that entire abstinence from sex was perhaps their best response; and Paul's castigation of 'the flesh', misunderstood, was pressed into the service of this disgust. So it came to be widely believed, in the Eastern churches first, and then in the West, that the 'perfect' Christian life was lived by monks and nuns in chastity; and that marriage, though necessary for the procreation of children, was only a second best. With it often went the view, certainly not Christian, but backed by selected biblical texts, that woman is the cause of sexual desire and of the consequent evil: did not Eve seduce Adam, not the other way round (what a weak man Adam was if this was so!)?

The great Augustine, Bishop of Hippo in North Africa early in the fifth century, put this view into theological form, and has exercised a magisterial influence, in this as in other matters, over all succeeding centuries. Before his conversion to Christianity he had lived a fashionably immoral life; in revulsion from it he joined the Manichees, who taught that all material things, including sex, were created by an evil deity. In the end he did not find their main doctrines convincing, and left them for the Neo-Platonists, who by no means went to the extremes of the Manichees, but had no great regard for the life of the flesh in comparison with the life of the spirit; and a few years later, converted by the preaching and teaching of Ambrose, Bishop of Milan, he became a Christian. As we look back on his pilgrimage we cannot be surprised that he brought with him into Christianity some of the ethical and theological baggage that he had accumulated on the way; the remarkable thing is that he brought so little. But he did bring with him his revulsion from sex.

He taught that the sin of Adam and Eve was sexual; that it is through the sexual act that sin is transmitted by generation after generation down to the present; that though sex within marriage is permissible for the procreation of children, it is sinful to enjoy it or to indulge in it for any purpose other than that of procreation; and that adultery or any sex outside marriage is an abomination.

This view prevailed in the church until the Reformation, and in large parts of the church after the Reformation also. The Reformers themselves modified it to the extent of showing that marriage is as honourable an estate as celibacy – in fact, usually more so – but they still left sex as the source of nearly all evil, with marriage as the only remedy. Adultery, of course, remained a terrible sin.

This harsh view of sex was toned down by many Christian teachers from the eighteenth century onwards, but its effects were felt well into our own century. Not only were many sexual inhibitions created and stoutly defended, but, more seriously still, sex itself came to be viewed in a quite unnatural light. It was something extra to human experience which came from an evilly insidious source, but could be dealt with on its own, by being denied or controlled. It was the plain duty of the Christian to avoid all reference to it, and to exclude it from his or her life except on certain legitimate occasions.

No wonder there was a 'sexual revolution' in the 1960s! The walls guarding 'Victorian morality', long eroded, were cast down; inhibitions were exposed and released; everything was permissible in the 'permissive society'. Reaction against the church's teaching was not entirely responsible for this. The widespread influence of Sigmund Freud (though his teaching was frequently misinterpreted), of Bertrand Russell (who reduced sex to a triviality), and of commercial interests in the media, all played their part. But the church also must bear part of the blame, if blame is to be apportioned, because of the constant immersion of its head in the sand.

The sexual revolution was by no means entirely bad. It called into question and disposed of views and prejudices about the relationship of men and women which claim to be Christian but have no real support in the teaching of the Bible, views which are hostile to the growth of true personality; it restored, unknowingly, the Old Testament view that sexual intercourse can be a matter for joy and celebration, not guilt or a grim sense of duty.

Its chief aim, certainly, was to increase the sum of human happiness. Here it lamentably failed. Adultery, now regarded as normal, whether engaged in because a marriage partner is not mature enough to sustain a stable, loving relationship, or because of a marriage breakdown, or at the urge of an ungovernable passion, or just for the sake of excitement, has not set people free from guilty feelings, and it still causes grievous hurt to many people: the partner thus rejected, the children involved, and often one or other of the adulterous couple. Moreover the permissibility of adultery has led, in part, to the other sexual problems of our time, the increase of prostitution, casual fornication, rape, child abuse, and pornography, and to the worst evil of all, the return to thinking of women as sex objects, as things not persons, just at the time when we could claim that the modern view of women as persons in their own right was beginning to prevail.

This long and painful history springs in part from the church's misunderstanding of the teaching of Jews. While the churches cling, if only subconsciously, to Augustinian views of sex, they have little chance of restoring the sexual balance which has gone so badly wrong.

But if they are willing to go behind Augustine to the Bible, and to state openly that we are sexual beings, as truly as we are rational beings, and that our sexuality is an integral part of our personhood as we have been created by God, and infuses all our activities and intentions; and if they go on to say that the basic objection to adultery, and to the other forms of sexual misconduct, is not the infringement of a property nor physical defilement but the flagrant breach of the commandment to love our neighbour as ourselves, that is, to love them as real persons, then they will have something constructive to say, first to their own bewildered members, trying to live in the Kingdom of God, and then to our sex-ridden society; at the same time they will be able to show mercy and understanding to those who in their search for self-fulfilment have fallen victims to the sexual fashions of our time, and found themselves all too often, inexorably, in the predicament of divorce, loneliness and bitterness. For they will have raised the whole issue of sexual relations above the taboos, the protests against conventional morality, the exhibitionism and the furtiveness which bedevil it to the level where, for the Christian, it belongs.

13 'You shall not steal'

As we embark on the study of the last three commandments, we may expect plainer sailing than we have so far experienced. The prohibition of stealing is to be found in every code of laws of which we have any knowledge, although it is said that in classical times the boys of Sparta were taught how to steal successfully as a preparation for military service in later life.

Modern commercialized, industrial society has added myriad ways of stealing to those known to the human race since primaeval times, from deceiving the Inland Revenue to insider dealing, from crime organized by the Mafia to profiteering on tickets to Wimbledon. But legislation in every country has to keep up with new devices as they are invented – though not always successfully – and the conscience of the human race is still unanimous in its insistence on the Eighth Commandment.

The Decalogue itself, moreover, on this point goes beyond itself, and in the Tenth Commandment, at which we shall arrive in due course, seeks to control the inner motivation of the outward act of stealing.

So it would seem that the Gospel has nothing to add to the wisdom of Moses. But it has. What it does is to include acquisitiveness and possessiveness within the concept of theft. 'Do not store up for yourselves treasure on earth, where it grows rusty and moth-eaten, and thieves break in to steal it' (Matt. 6.19). 'If a man wants to sue you for your shirt, let him have your coat as well ... Give when you are asked to give; and do not turn your back on a man who wants to borrow' (Matt. 5.38–42). That is, in the Kingdom of God we are not to hold on to our possessions, but to give them away to anyone in need. There is no suggestion that the Rich Young Ruler had acquired his possessions by dishonest methods; nevertheless for the sake of the Kingdom he was to sell them and give away the proceeds to the poor (Mark 10.17–22). There is no suggestion that those who store up treasure on earth are necessarily rogues; nevertheless in the Kingdom of God treasure is not to be stored up. And Jesus has no hesitation in telling us that it is virtually impossible for a rich man to enter the Kingdom (Mark 10.24) – a statement not often quoted by those who hold that obedience to Christ brings success in business.

Something even more seductive than wealth comes within the scope of this teaching. Wealth, as is well-known, is usually valued not for itself but for the power which it brings with it; and power is something which most people aim at – by fair or unfair means – and something which few people are willing to give up when they have gained it (even when, perhaps especially when, it is only power over a son or daughter or wife or husband). 'What we have, we hold' is a motto which commands widespread agreement and even admiration. There are very few, if any, examples in history of the voluntary giving up of power – of bigger nations over smaller nations, of one class over another class, of one race over another race, of the rich over the poor, of one sex over the other. In Britain we like to think that we gave up the rule of India and of the rest of the Empire voluntarily, but while the voluntary element was prominent in the minds of some high-minded people, it is very doubtful if we would have surrendered the Empire without a large amount of duress.

Churchpeople and their leaders have not often proved to be exceptions to this rule. There can be a struggle for power 'at the top', although those engaged in it may proffer excellent reasons for their course of action (and even deceive themselves); there can be a struggle for power about the secretaryship of a local committee. Those who possess power, or status, or prestige, have been known to hold on to it long after they have ceased to be the best person to hold it. The dominance of the male in church life is the clearest example of all. And whole churches, throughout Christian history, can be held guilty of the same offence. It sometimes seems that union schemes are likely to succeed only when all the parties to it are of roughly equal power and status, and, therefore, as is sometimes openly said, 'have nothing to lose'.

But 'the Son of Man did not come to be served, but to serve, and to give up his life as a ransom for many' (Mark 10.43), and the same spirit of self-abrogation is required of all those who belong to the Kingdom.

But there is a grave dilemma concealed in all this which must now be brought into the open. It arises, once again, from the fact that the Kingdom of God is placed in the middle of a society which does not accept its principles. In an ideal society wealth, if required at all, and it would probably be required, would be fairly shared by all ('to each according to his need'), and the exercise of power would not be necessary, for everyone would willingly obey the laws. There would no doubt be people who organized the traffic and collected contributions etc., but they would not need the force of law behind them. But in the actual society in which we live there has to be power, to deter and apprehend villains and to enforce obedience to the laws.

Should those who do not believe in the possession of power stand aside, and let those exercise it who do believe in it? It is safe to say that if this were to happen, those who have power would take it eagerly, and exercise it, and hold on to it; and they are precisely the people who should not be trusted with power. The inactivity of the good would unleash the ambitions of the not-so-good. Therefore we have to say that those who do not desire power must be asked to hold it; those who believe in being power*less* have to become power*ful*. But this will be in the firm hope that they will use their power for the common good, and relinquish it when they have done all that they can. Thus 'the principle of good compromise' will have come into effective operation.

When good people come into power, determined to use it well, they are not, however, immune from the temptation to value it for

its own sake. Nor from the desire to use it for the purpose of gaining their own ends, or for imposing their own views on the community, no doubt in the belief that their ends are for everyone's
welfare, and that their views are correct. To them Jesus says in the
Beatitudes: 'How blest are those of a gentle spirit; they shall have
the earth for their possession.' Gentleness, or meekness (to use the
translation in the older versions), is not weakness or false humility,
or a willingness always to give way, or a softness of approach. It is
the quality of those who have ability, or power, and use it, not to
get their own way, but to serve the interests of others and bring out
in others the abilities which they have. Such people genuinely will
'have the earth for their possession' (or 'inherit the earth', as we may
prefer to say): for they are the only people who possess without
becoming possessive, and inherit without becoming acquisitive.
They enjoy the whole earth, because they threaten no one and covet
nothing.

'You shall not steal,' and in the Kingdom you do not hold on
grimly to the power or wealth that you have, but use them to build
up and encourage and enrich the lives of others; that is the positive
meaning of the Eighth Commandment.

14 'You shall not give false evidence against your neighbour'

Presumably it is equally wrong to give false evidence *for* one's neighbour!

Moses, we are told, was criticized by his father-in-law for sitting in court all day to judge every law suit brought by any Israelite; and advised by him to set up a permanent lower court of 'capable, God-fearing, honest and incorruptible men' which would judge simple cases and refer difficult ones to himself as the supreme judge. Moses took this advice (Ex. 18.13–27).

If this is a reliable tradition, as it may well be, it shows the importance attached to legal justice from the very first days of the Israelite nation. Legal justice requires the prevention of false evidence, together with the ability of the judge to decide between different accounts of the same event.

The impartiality of the courts and their ability to find out the truth constitute one of the foundations of ordered society. They cannot perform their functions if the evidence given to them is false; so the detection and punishment of perjury are essential prerequisites of justice. If the suspicion gains ground that perjury is undetected and unpunished, in Jerusalem, Rome, Gibraltar, South Africa, Ulster or London, society begins to rock on its foundations.

The Ninth Commandment needs no further justification than this, and has never been felt to require it.

The Gospels give no direct indication of the way in which this

Commandment may need reinterpretation in the Kingdom of God, though they tell us that Jesus himself was condemned on false evidence by the Sanhedrin (Mark 14.57–58). But we shall not go far wrong if we extend the veto on false evidence beyond the courtroom to all human relationships, and at the same time change it from being merely negative into being positive as well. 'You shall not tell lies about your neighbour; you shall tell the truth about your neighbour.'

Lies about our neighbour are of many different kinds. They take the form of slander or libel, in which case they can be brought under the judgment of the courts, usually at great and often impossible expense. Newspapers keep lawyers on hand to advise them how far they can go in suggesting what may turn out to be untrue without incurring legal proceedings; and have funds in reserve in case their lawyers give the wrong advice.

But most lies are told in malicious gossip, not amounting to a legal offence, or in the attempt to downgrade our neighbours in the eyes of others. Many consist not in downright false statements, but in innuendoes, and in the omission of relevant facts with overemphasis on those which tell against the victim.

We can also lie about ourselves. The biggest lie is to pretend to be what we are not.

To tell the positive truth about our neighbour is often more difficult than refraining from lies about him or her. It requires a knowledge not only of the facts, but of motivations and circumstances, both the obvious and the concealed ones; and of the pressures, and the mental and physical limitations, by which he or she is constrained. It requires compassion and understanding as well as knowledge. It is, in fact, an eminent example of loving our neighbours as ourselves, for we certainly give great attention, not to say indulgence, to ourselves, to our motivations, circumstances, pressures and limitations, as we seek to understand and, if possible, justify ourselves. Our neighbours call for nothing less, and nothing more, than we give ourselves. We are to speak the truth in love (Eph. 4.15).

But here we hit on a snag. It is obvious that politicians, diplomats, advertisers, doctors and certain journalists in the pay of newspaper magnates by no means always speak 'the truth, the whole truth and nothing but the truth'. They claim the right, sometimes explicitly, to be 'economical with the truth'. We may hope – sometimes with reasonable confidence, sometimes not – that they overstate or under-state, or conceal, or simply evade the question, in the interests of a greater good even than truth, such as the public welfare, and not for financial or party-political reasons. Certainly this is to be expected from those of them who claim to be Christians, or are otherwise committed to truth-telling.

Are ordinary Christians permitted the same licence? It may well be that they are, since to tell the truth outright about people is some-times to hurt, to discourage, even to drive to distraction or suicide, those to whom or about whom it is told. It can be a failure in love to blurt out the whole truth. Equally it may be a failure in love to withhold the truth indefinitely. There is no dilemma which calls for a more discerning exercise of the 'principle of good compromise'.

'You shall not covet your neighbour's house — wife, slave, slave-girl, ox, ass or anything that belongs to him'

If there were any doubt whether the Seventh Commandment implies that a wife is her husband's property, the Tenth Commandment (which is probably a good deal later than the time of Moses) would put this doubt to rest. A man's wife simply appears in a list of his belongings, without any rights or personality of her own.

It is probable, as we have seen, that the status of wives improved somewhat in the course of Jewish history before the time of Christ. In Proverbs (31.10ff.) (to be dated about 300 BC, we are told) we read: 'Who can find a capable wife? Her worth is far beyond coral. Her husband's whole trust is in her . . . She repays him with good, not evil, all her life long . . . After careful thought she buys a field; and plants a vineyard out of her earnings . . . When she opens her mouth, it is to speak wisely, and loyalty is the theme of her teaching.' This passage certainly shows a considerable advance, but even here it is evident that a wife's legal rights are very slight. And the notion of the wife as property still underlies the law of divorce at the time of Christ: by Jewish law only the husband could divorce.

For our purposes, however, we can happily exclude our neighbour's wife from the schedule of property attached to the Tenth Commandment - and indeed, for various reasons, all the other items, except his house, as well - and will in fact do best to reduce it to the simple prescription: 'You shall not covet your neighbour's property.'

Thus reduced to its fundamental principle, the Commandment is still accepted and acceptable as part of the moral law. It cannot be part of legal justice since it does not refer to the outward act of misappropriation, but only to the inward motive that may or may not lead to it. It has often been pointed out that it is the only one of the Ten of which this is true. (Some scholars indeed say that the word translated 'covet' means 'attempt to acquire'; but this would make the Tenth Commandment into a virtual repetition of the Eighth.)

The gospel of the Kingdom assumes and confirms the Tenth Commandment; and agrees with the moral law that the desire to steal, if entertained and nourished, is as wrong as the act of stealing itself. But the gospel goes on to extend and deepen the area of human life where covetousness is to be found and countered. Our desire for other people's possessions takes two forms: we covet what we can conceivably, under certain circumstances, take away from our neighbour, legally or illegally. This desire is covered by the Commandment. We also covet what we know we cannot take away from him or her, but nevertheless desire to have – our neighbour's brain-power, position in society or in business, artistic talents, charm, wisdom, goodness, etc. etc. The other name for the second kind of covetousness is envy; and Paul tells us in the passage where he most truly expresses the spirit of the gospel: 'Love envies no one' (I Cor. 13.4). This is the Tenth Commandment in the Kingdom of God.

Envy boils up within us and leads inevitably to the bad kind of competitiveness. The gospel does not prohibit the development of our own gifts. On the contrary: we are to love our neighbour as ourself, and therefore we are to love ourself as we love our neighbour; we are nowhere instructed to give priority to one love over the other (except that there are so many neighbours that we may not have much time for loving ourself!). But competitiveness is another matter. It may be comparatively harmless, of course, in the cases where envy is not encouraged and dies away; but it can also be wholly destructive, mentally, spiritually and physically.

A particularly pernicious form it can take is the urgent desire to make more money, drive better and faster cars, live in more splendid houses, than our rivals, and especially those who are neighbours in the strictly literal sense. But it is not limited to the 'upwardly mobile'; it is found, in one form or another, at every level of society. The temptation is particularly insidious because competitiveness of every kind is regarded by the majority of people as perfectly reputable, especially in the enterprise culture in which we now live.

Genuine delight in the happiness or success of others, added to contentment with one's own lot, when it cannot be improved, does not come automatically or easily. Indeed it sometimes seems to be one of the rarer gifts of the Spirit. But we are to 'be ambitious for the higher gifts' (I Cor. 12.31 RSV).

Epilogue

Those who try to obey the laws of the Kingdom in such a society as ours cannot exempt themselves from its business, its industry, its trade and commerce and its political and educational structure. On the contrary, they are to exercise a positive role within it. That role is to remind our contemporaries, by example, of the possibility and claims of an 'alternative society' – a society in which wealth is created for the benefit of all, and not of the few, and in which individuals and groups of people develop and exercise their gifts, not to aggrandize themselves in wealth, power and prestige, but to serve the human family, world-wide.

Such a society does not exist, and has never existed. Its coming-into-existence will require change in human attitudes, a vast store of goodwill and mutual trust, the working out of innumerable details, a global concept of education, and political and financial measures of a far-reaching kind. There is no guarantee that it will ever become real. But there is no escape for those who love God with all their heart and mind and strength and their neighbours as themselves from living by its laws in the power of the Spirit.